RAND | NATIONAL DEFENSE RESEARCH INSTITUTE

The Role of Special and Incentive Pays in Retaining Military Mental Health Care Providers

James Hosek, Shanthi Nataraj, Michael G. Mattock, Beth J. Asch

Prepared for the Office of the Secretary of Defense

For more information on this publication, visit www.rand.org/t/RR1425

Library of Congress Cataloging-in-Publication Data
ISBN: 978-0-8330-9489-6

Published by the RAND Corporation, Santa Monica, Calif.
© Copyright 2017 RAND Corporation
RAND® is a registered trademark.

*Cover: Sgt. Christopher Calvert, 1st Air Calvary Brigade 1st
Calvary Division Public Affairs.*

Support RAND
Make a tax-deductible charitable contribution at
www.rand.org/giving/contribute

www.rand.org

Preface

Officer special and incentive (S&I) pays are used to create incentives for officer retention to meet manning requirements. No capability exists to assess how alternative S&I pay adjustments affect the retention of mental health care officers, however, and as a result policymakers lack an analytical and empirical basis for determining the effect of such adjustments on retention. This report, requested by the Office of Compensation with the Office of the Secretary of Defense, Personnel and Readiness, responds to the need for such a basis for military mental health care providers. The report should interest policymakers responsible for setting and adjusting military compensation and maintaining military health care capability.

This research was conducted within the Forces and Resources Policy Center of the RAND National Defense Research Institute, a federally funded research and development center sponsored by the Office of the Secretary of Defense, the Joint Staff, the Unified Combatant Commands, the Navy, the Marine Corps, the defense agencies, and the defense Intelligence Community.

For more information on the Forces and Resources Policy Center, see www.rand.org/nsrd/ndri/centers/frp or contact the director (contact information is provided on the web page).

Contents

Figures

Tables

Summary

After more than a decade of war, the military services have many returning personnel with mental health needs, and thus the United States needs to ensure that it has the capacity to address their needs. The objective of this research is to create a capability for predicting the effect of changes in the type or amount of special and incentive (S&I) pays on the retention of officers in mental health professions.

We used RAND's dynamic retention model (DRM) as the analytical basis for relating S&I pays to retention. The DRM is a dynamic programming model of individual retention and reserve component participation over the life cycle in a world with uncertainty and with individual preferences for military service. Several steps were needed to implement the DRM for mental health care professionals. We reviewed financial aid programs covering education costs offered by the military and developed an approach for conceptualizing and modeling the choice of financial aid with associated service obligations. Estimation of the model requires information on expected military and civilian pay over a career, as well as longitudinal data on active duty retention and subsequent participation, if any, in the reserve components. We reviewed S&I pays and used regular military compensation plus the expected amount of scheduled S&I pays by year of service to develop expected military pay by year of service for each occupation. We used American Community Survey data to estimate civilian earnings regressions and predict expected earnings by age and earnings decile, by occupation. We also modified the DRM to handle the service member's choice of obligation length under multiyear special pay.

We used the estimates of expected military and civilian pay and the modified DRM to estimate DRM parameters for psychiatrists, psychologists, nurses, mental health care nurses, occupational therapists pooled with physician assistants, and social workers. The data used in estimation covered officer entry cohorts into active duty from 1990 through 2000 followed through 2010 for officers "entering" at the O-3 level. Nearly all parameter estimates were statistically significant, and the estimated models fit the data well.

Finally, with the estimated models and code developed for policy simulation, we demonstrated a capability to simulate the steady-state retention effects of counterfactual changes in S&I pays. This capability can be applied to predict the effect of alternative levels and types of S&I pays, including those that entail the service member to commit to a certain number of additional years of service. Further, the approach taken here can be used to update the model in the future and take advantage of an increased sample size, and it may be possible to extend the model in promising directions—for example, to consider the impact of special pays on a future officer's decision to enter a mental health care occupation, or the impact of the pace of military operations the retention of these officers.

Acknowledgments

We appreciate the support and guidance offered by Jeri Busch, director, Office of Compensation (Office of the Secretary of Defense, Personnel and Readiness), and Bill Dougherty, Steve Galing, Pat Mulcahy, and Don Svendsen of the Office of Compensation. At RAND, Arthur Bullock assisted in database creation, Sarah Bana helped gather information about S&I pays, and Whitney Dudley and Mark Totten provided research programming for civilian and military wage analysis. We thank Craig A. Bond and Edward G. Keating for their reviews of this work.

CHAPTER ONE

Introduction

The military operations in Iraq and Afghanistan have exposed many service members to stressful and traumatic experiences that affect mental health. Spouses have been stressed by repercussions from service members' stress and the responsibility to manage household affairs and finances during the member's deployment cycle, and stressed children have exhibited a higher incidence of emotional and behavioral problems. The Department of Defense Task Force on Mental Health (2007), in discussing the need to ensure an adequate supply of uniformed care givers, recommended that the department "review and increase the effectiveness of incentives to attract and retain highly-qualified active duty mental health professionals."

At present, policymakers do not have a capability to predict the retention effects of special and incentive (S&I) pays for mental health professionals, and the purpose of this research is to develop such a capability. The capability we develop is based on a theory of retention over a career, empirically grounded, and capable of predicting the effect of changes in S&I pays even though the changes might be beyond those observed historically.

The following occupations are covered in the analysis (this list is based on Robiner's [2006] definition of *mental health care provider*[1]):

- psychiatrist
- psychologist
- registered nurse
- physician assistant
- occupational therapist
- social worker.

Method of Analysis

We use RAND's dynamic retention model (DRM) as the conceptual basis of retention over a career. The DRM treats individual decisionmaking about whether to stay or leave the military as a stochastic dynamic programming problem. An individual on active duty in a given point

---

[1] Robiner (2006) defines occupations related to mental health care as including psychiatry, psychology, psychiatric nursing, social work, marriage and family therapy, mental health counseling, substance abuse counseling, and occupational therapy. As we discuss in later chapters, we estimate our model with military personnel data for the cohorts entering active service between 1990 and 2000. For our entry cohorts, the military did not have specific occupational codes for psychiatric nursing, marriage and family therapy, mental health counseling, and substance abuse counseling. Consequently, we were required to use the more aggregated occupational codes in our study.

in his or her career evaluates the value of staying versus leaving. If the individual decides to leave, he or she works in the civilian economy and each year can decide whether to participate in the reserve components or not.

The values of staying in the military or leaving depend on financial and nonfinancial factors. The financial factors reflect expected military and civilian compensation. Nonfinancial factors are represented by random shocks that occur on both the military and civilian sides and by individual preferences, or tastes, for military service, which differ across individuals. The values of staying or leaving also depend on the option value arising from being able to stay on active duty or leave in future periods if the decision in the current period is to stay.

The DRM is not simply a conceptual model. Its parameters are estimated with data on officer retention and reserve participation, giving the model an empirical grounding. Inputs into the estimation include information on expected military and civilian earnings over a career, which we develop. We use the estimated DRM to demonstrate its capability to simulate the retention effect of changes in S&I pays.

Recent Literature

Several studies examine physician retention in the military, although none take a full-career perspective. Keating et al. (2009a, 2009b) document retention rates among Air Force physicians and show that annual attrition rates were around 12 percent between 1980 and 2000 and trended down from 2000 to 2006. They find that physicians who entered the Air Force after completing their residency exhibited high attrition rates at the third and fourth years of service, when they first became eligible to make a stay-leave decision. In contrast, physicians who entered the military without having completed their residency—typically because they were participating in a military residency program—remained in service longer. The authors examine the relationship between the amount of Multiyear Special Pay (MSP) offered for a four-year commitment and whether a physician accepts an MSP offer and stays in the Air Force. Controlling for individual characteristics and physician specialty, they find that higher MSP offers are associated with higher acceptance rates of four-year MSP. The acceptance rate at the end of the active duty service obligation (ADSO) is approximately 15 percent for a $20,000 four-year MSP (in 2007 dollars) and 25 percent for a $40,000 four-year MSP.

Mundell (2010) models cumulative duration on active duty among physicians in all services as a function of physician and job characteristics. He finds that job-related characteristics are related to retention. Physicians stationed at larger medical centers, which offer more specialty practice opportunities within the military, have lower attrition. The occurrence of deployment during an initial service obligation period increases attrition, but deployment after an initial obligation period decreases attrition among who remain beyond the initial obligation.

Hogan et al. (2012) compare the number of personnel in mental health occupations during fiscal year (FY) 2010 with the number of authorized personnel. Personnel levels are around 90 percent of authorizations overall, though the Navy had the lowest personnel-to-authorizations ratios. Annual retention rates for mental health providers are generally above 80 percent as a cohort moves from one year of service to the next, although rates dip in the years when individuals in each occupation are likely to have completed their initial active duty service obligations. The authors project that a 25 percent increase in the amount of MSP offered for a four-year contract would increase psychiatrist retention rates between year of service (YOS) 7 and YOS 16, thus decreasing the number of accessions needed to meet FY 2015 authorizations by about 18 percent (from 287 to 236 accessions). Introducing a graduated retention bonus for social workers up to $10,000 per year for a four-year commitment would decrease accession requirements through FY 2015 by three in the Navy out of a projected 87 and by 11 in the Air Force out of a projected 122. Moreover, the authors estimate that increasing the selective retention bonus by two award levels for Navy enlisted mental health specialists would decrease accession requirements through FY 2015 by 102.

Gray and Grefer (2012) distinguish retention in three segments of a physician's military career: the first year after completing service obligations associated with the physician's medical school and residency programs; the years after this up to retirement eligibility at YOS 20; and the first year of retirement eligibility. The authors estimate the probability of staying as a function of the present value of the difference between expected military and civilian pay, ADSO, and individual and service-related characteristics. The authors note that while pay affects retention, retention may also affect pay; for example, the military may increase incentive pays for physicians in response to low retention rates. To address this, the authors use regular military compensation (RMC) and retirement benefits as an instrument for the pay differential, arguing that RMC is a valid instrument because it is correlated with the pay differential but not correlated with unobserved factors that induce higher incentive pay. Mean annual retention is 28 percent in the first unobligated YOS, 88 percent in the period from this year to YOS 19, and 75 percent in YOS 20. The estimates suggest that a 10 percent increase in RMC would increase retention by nearly 19 percent in the first unobligated YOS, less than 0.5 percent between that year and YOS 19, and almost 4 percent in YOS 20.

Ritschard et al. (2011) report on data from a survey of current and former military psychiatrists and psychologists. The survey covered military experiences, satisfaction with military service, and retention incentives. Respondents included 198 psychiatrists and 163 psychologists on active duty. About 50 percent of psychiatrists and 70 percent of psychologists reported being satisfied, very satisfied, or extremely satisfied. Respondents also included 20 psychiatrists and 10 psychologists no longer in the military. In addition, 13 former Public Health Service officers completed the survey. Most former psychiatrists reported not being satisfied with their experience as a military health care provider, though most psychologists reported being satisfied. Current and former providers were asked to rate various aspects of military service. For both groups, the highest-rated aspects included mental health care treatment practices, mental health provider camaraderie, and leadership opportunities. Mental health care management and administrative policies, morale among mental health providers, and the provision of administrative support staff were among the lowest-rated aspects. Top-rated incentives in both groups included counting bonus pay toward retirement benefits, counting graduate medical education toward time served, shorter and fewer deployments, and promotion criteria that emphasize clinical skills. Current active duty members also mentioned increased bonuses and basic pay and reduced administrative duties.

Our work contributes to this literature by modeling retention decisions over the entire military career with time-consistent decisionmaking and allowing for heterogeneity in tastes and shocks both within and outside the military. Through its explicit decisionmaking paradigm, dynamic programming, the DRM allows individuals to re-optimize their decisions in each future period as particular conditions are realized. Further, because the estimated model identifies population parameters—namely, the mean and variance of active and reserve tastes, the variances of shocks, and the personal discount factor—the estimated model can be used for counterfactual analyses that reveal how a simulated but representative population would behave. These analyses show the effect of a change in S&I pay on retention over a career. Further, following Mattock and Arkes (2007), the DRM models the individual's choice over MSP offers requiring multiyear service commitments. This allows us to simulate the retention effects of changing the structure and amount of MSP.

Organization of This Report

Chapter Two describes military financial aid programs for physicians. Chapter Three discusses the financial aid choice and presents the DRM. Chapters Four and Five describe the military and civilian pay lines for health professionals that are used as inputs when estimating the DRM. Chapter Six describes the method of estimation and data and presents parameter estimates and goodness of fit, and Chapter Seven presents simulations of the effects on retention of hypothetical changes in S&I pays. Chapter Eight offers our conclusions.

CHAPTER TWO

Military Financial Aid Programs for Physicians

Financial aid to cover the cost of medical education is an appealing incentive to attract physicians into the military. The military offers several sources of financial aid for medical education. These are the Health Professions Scholarship Program (HPSP), the Financial Assistance Program (FAP), the Uniformed Services University of the Health Sciences (USUHS), and the Active Duty Health Professions Loan Repayment Program (ADHPLRP). Each type of aid entails an ADSO. USUHS is a military medical school that charges its students no tuition and pays a salary at the level of a beginning officer, O-1. The choice to attend USUHS is made during the application and admissions process. HPSP is chosen at entry into or during medical school (other than USUHS). FAP is financial assistance for those who have completed medical school and are in, or plan to enter, a civilian residency. ADHPLRP is for fully trained physicians—those who have completed medical school and a residency program—who enter the military. We discuss the choice among programs in the next chapter, where Table 3.1 summarizes the programs. In some cases, there are counterparts to these programs for other health care professionals, such as nurses and physician assistants, and we mention these in our discussion. Finally, financial aid is separate from the S&I pays for health professionals, which are discussed in Chapter Four.

In addition to describing the cost of medical school and the military financial aid packages for physicians, we recognize in our discussion that the attractiveness of each type of financial aid may depend on the physician's taste for military service. We explore selectivity to some extent in Chapter Six by estimating separate models for psychiatrists entering via USUHS versus HPSP.

Cost of Medical School

Military financial aid helps to cover the cost of medical school. For the 2013–2014 academic year, the out-of-pocket cost of attending medical school ranged from $58,000 to $77,000 for the median student. Tuition, fees, and health insurance at public medical schools totaled $33,220 for in-state residents and $56,998 for out-of-state residents, and at private medical schools totaled $52,000 (see Association of American Medical Colleges, 2015b). Living expenses were roughly $25,000 per year. Based on these numbers, four years of medical school costs ranged from $232,000 to $308,000.

Eighty-three percent of the medical school class of 2015 had education debt. Median indebtedness in 2015 was $180,000 at public medical schools and $200,000 at private medical schools. The overall median of debt was $183,000, and 79 percent of those with debt had debt of $100,000 or more, 45 percent had $200,000 or more, and 12 percent had $300,000 or more (Association of American Medical Colleges, 2015a). The difference between the cost of medical school and the debt, $50,000 to over $100,000, was financed by means other than debt—e.g., own savings and earnings, parental transfers, and scholarships.

Students typically enter a residency program for graduate medical education after medical school. The first year of the program, the internship, is necessary for a license to practice medicine. Many residency programs are three to five years long, depending on specialty; the psychiatry residency is four years. Online estimates of residency salary, or stipend, show a 2013 median of $59,100 (Payscale.com, 2016) and an average of about $60,000 (SalaryExpert.com, 2016). According to data from the Association of American Medical Colleges, the 2015 median stipend was $52,000 in the first year and increased to $58,100 in the fourth year of residency (Association of American Medical Colleges, 2015a), numbers that were a bit lower than the online estimates we found.

Military Financial Aid Programs

Our discussion focuses on HPSP, FAP, USUHS, and ADHPLRP.

Health Professions Scholarship Program

HPSP is available to qualified students in accredited medical, dental, optometry, veterinary, psychiatric nurse practitioner, and clinical or counseling psychology programs (GoArmy.com, no date). It pays school tuition, fees, a monthly stipend, and an allowance for books and equipment. Individuals participate in 45 days of training each year as inactive reserve officers. The ADSO is a minimum of two years for Army physicians (AR 601-141, 2006) and three years for Air Force and Navy physicians, and one year of duty for each year of aid after the minimum (Navy Medicine, no date).[1] HPSP pays a monthly stipend for nine months; the stipend was $2,157 in 2013. The 45 days of reserve service are paid at the O-1 level of basic pay, $2,876 a month in 2013, plus subsistence and housing allowances. The subsistence allowance was $224 per month in 2013, and the partial housing allowance (for a reservist living in government-furnished housing and with 30 or more consecutive days of duty) was $13.20 per month. The monthly stipend and reserve pay totaled $24,000 per year. Medical school tuition and fees were also paid, so pay and direct aid under HPSP covered practically all of the annual cost of medical school. Also, there can be an HPSP accession bonus of up to $20,000 (GoArmy.com, no date).

HPSP recipients must apply for a military residency program and may apply for a waiver to pursue a civilian residency.[2] The psychiatry residency is four years and incurs a three-year

---

[1] Navy recipients who also have an accession bonus have a minimum four-year ADSO that may be served concurrently with the HPSP ADSO.

[2] A useful guide to the HPSP program is the *HPSP Medical Student Survival Guide* (U.S. Department of Defense, Department of the Air Force, Department of the Navy, and Department of the Army, 2013). It does not discuss the criteria for granting waivers for a civilian residency but advises medical students to be competitive for selection: ". . . always maximize your likelihood to be selected for your specialty choice, whether for active duty or civilian training." Selection for military and civilian residencies within a specialty is based on individual competitiveness relative to other candidates and takes into account the individual's preferred rankings of residencies. The available number of military residencies is a factor in selection.

ADSO if it is a military residency—but, notably, the HPSP and military residency ADSOs can be served concurrently. A civilian residency does not incur an ADSO. The time spent in a civilian residency is countable as years of service in determining pay when one enters the military; if it were not countable, civilian residents would be disadvantaged at entry relative to their military residency peers. By the same token, by allowing the ADSOs for HPSP and military residency to be served concurrently, a military resident is not disadvantaged relative to a civilian resident. If the ADSOs had to be served sequentially, the military resident would be disadvantaged. The military has only a limited number of residency slots, and as a result there may be a good chance for a civilian residency. Mundell's (2010) Tables 5.2 to 5.4 indicate that at most military medical treatment facilities more than half of the psychiatrists in the military in the past decade had a civilian residency.

Military residents start active duty as O-3s. Civilian residents are not on active duty and do not receive military compensation but do receive a residency stipend. Regular military compensation in 2013 for an O-3 with less than two years of service was $6,010 per month, or $72,124 per year. Also, the time spent in a military residency counts toward eligibility for military retirement. By comparison, the median civilian residency stipend was $50,000 to $56,000 per year (see above), or about $16,000 to $20,000 less than military compensation. For further information on the earnings of residents and fellows, we reviewed more than 20 Internet sites using the search terms "medical residency salary" and "medical fellowship salary." Most residents received a salary of $50,000 to $60,000, depending on pay grade. Residency pay tables typically have seven grades, and pay increases by about $1,500 from one grade to the next. Fellowships offer a little more, up to $68,000. The data suggest that offers are higher in cities with higher costs of living: An offer might be $54,000 in Boston versus $49,000 in Nashville. Residents and fellows work long hours. A number of institutional sites (e.g., hospitals) limit working hours to no more than 80 hours per week and restrict moonlighting by requiring permission from the residency program to do so.

The policy setting is somewhat different in the Navy than the Army and Air Force. HPSP recipients must apply for a Navy internship and may request a waiver for a civilian internship and residency. For those with a Navy internship, during the internship individuals may apply for a military residency or civilian residency, apply for flight surgery, apply for undersea medicine, or request a general medical officer (GMO) tour with the Marine Corps or Navy. The GMO tour is typically two or three years. Time spent on a GMO tour is active duty creditable toward the HPSP ADSO. But because a GMO tour occurs before a military residency, if any, GMO years cannot concurrently repay a residency ADSO—there is no residency ADSO yet. The Navy internship year counts against the HPSP *minimum* service obligation of three years, decreasing it to two years. However, it does not count against the HPSP ADSO per se, nor does it add to the ADSO. A person with a two-year HPSP (and a three-year minimum service obligation) could leave the Navy after a two-year GMO tour and seek a residency in a civilian hospital as a civilian. This person would spend a total of three years in the Navy, one year for the internship and two years for the GMO tour. A person with a three-year HPSP could do the internship and a two-year GMO tour but would still need to serve one more year of active duty.[3] This person would probably seek a three-year GMO tour if he or she wanted to

---

[3] The one-year internship would count against the three-year minimum service obligation. However, three years of HPSP create a three-year ADSO, so three years would have to be served. Note that the minimum service obligation and the ADSO, although related, are distinct quantities.

keep time in the military as short as possible, given the three-year HPSP. In the Army and Air Force, HPSP recipients must apply for a residency in their service and may request a waiver for a civilian residency (which would include an internship as the first year of the residency), but there is no option to apply for a GMO tour or other assignment in the field.

For examples of different paths, a four-year HPSP ADSO and a four-year military residency, which entails a three-year ADSO, are *concurrently* fulfilled with four years of active duty after the residency. If the residency is civilian, the ADSO is four years as a result of the HPSP. These examples might reflect paths in the Army, Navy, or Air Force. For the Navy, another possible path is a four-year HPSP, one-year Navy internship, two-year GMO tour, and a three-year Navy residency (not including the internship year). The two-year GMO tour repays two years of the four-year HPSP ADSO, and its remaining two years are paid in the first two years of the three years of service needed to repay the three-year residency. This path has nine years of active duty. Alternatively, if the residency is a three-year civilian residency, it generates no ADSO. The two-year GMO tour plus two additional years of service after the GMO tour would fulfill the four-year HPSP ADSO. In this case, there would be five years of active duty and eight years for the entire path (one year of internship, two years of GMO, three years of civilian residency, and two more years of active duty).

Financial Assistance Program

FAP is an opportunity to receive financial aid from the military for medical school graduates who did not apply for HPSP or were not approved for it. Some medical students might not have realized how much debt they would accumulate in medical school, and FAP could be a welcome source of money to pay off medical school loans. Others might have wanted to avoid the requirement to apply for a military residency; FAP does not require this, whereas HPSP does.

Eligibility for FAP requires that the individual be a medical school graduate, complete a one-year postgraduate program (medical internship), and be enrolled in an accredited medical residency or fellowship program. FAP is also available to dental students who are currently enrolled or accepted for an accredited residency or fellowship program.

FAP pays a monthly stipend plus an annual grant for tuition, fees, books, and equipment for training. FAP participants have 14 days of active duty training each year and are paid as an O-1. The monthly stipend in 2013 was $2,157, and the annual grant was $45,000. The monthly stipend, 14 days of O-1 pay, and the annual grant summed to $71,000.

FAP recipients are free to apply for a civilian residency, which pays a salary. Thus, the $71,000 from FAP could be applied during residency toward repaying medical school loans. Based on the medical school debt numbers cited above, four years of after-tax FAP dollars would repay the medical school debt of most medical school graduates.

The ADSO in the Army, Navy, and Air Force is the number of years of FAP plus one (e.g., five years of service for four years of FAP).[4] A three-year FAP recipient can fulfill the ADSO with four years of active duty service. A three-year HPSP recipient might spend four years in a military residency followed by four years of active duty to fulfill the ADSO, totaling eight years in the military.

---

[4] Navy FAP recipients incur a two-year ADSO for the first year of FAP and one year for each subsequent year, and have a minimum of three years of active service (Navy Medicine, no date). The Army and Air Force have a minimum of two years of active duty (U.S. Army Recruiting Command, 2013, p. 12; U.S. Air Force, no date).

Uniformed Services University of Health Sciences

USUHS is a fully accredited medical school that pays tuition and fees and provides textbooks for its students. The curriculum is two years of courses plus two years in clerkships at military hospitals. This four-year program comes with a seven-year ADSO plus six years in the Individual Ready Reserve. Students enter USUHS as commissioned officers at O-1 and stay at this level while they are USUHS medical students. Regular military compensation for an O-1 is $4,473 per month, or $53,673 per year. USUHS also offers graduate training.

USUHS medical school graduates promote to O-3 and do a one-year internship in their specialty area, e.g., psychiatry. USUHS calls this year Graduate Medical Education–1 (GME-1). It does not incur any ADSO and does not repay any of the seven-year ADSO. After this year,

> candidates not already selected for continuous training and seeking further specialty training are selected on a competitive basis for residency assignments depending on the needs of the medical departments. Graduates may be required to serve in operational assignments as general medical officers before becoming eligible for specialty or subspecialty training. . . . Time spent in residency training does not count toward satisfying the [seven-year ADSO] but is creditable in determining retirement eligibility. . . . [To] complete GME-1 and a residency program and fulfill all payback requirements, including the initial obligation for medical school, the average graduate spends approximately 11 years on active duty after receiving the M.D. degree. (Uniformed Services University of the Health Sciences, 2007)

For example, USUHS medical school is four years, GME-1 is one year, and a military residency is three years. Seven years of service after the residency pays off the USUHS ADSO. This example requires 11 years on active duty counting GME-1 and residency, after the four years at USUHS.

Some who attend USUHS are graduates of service academies. Attending a service academy incurs a six-year service obligation that must be served in addition to, not concurrently with, ADSOs from USUHS or HPSP. An obligation from Reserve Officers' Training Corps (ROTC) financial aid is also additive.

Active Duty Health Professions Loan Repayment Program.

ADHPLRP is an incentive for the direct accession (or retention) of fully qualified medical personnel. These are individuals who have completed medical school, internship, and residency and are licensed. A maximum annual award amount is "prescribed by law and adjusted each year by the percentage increase in the average annual cost of educational expenses and stipend costs of a single scholarship under AFHPSP/FAP" (AR 601-141, 2006). The maximum award was $120,000 in 2013, payable at $40,000 per year for up to three years. The repayment may cover "loans amounts for principal, interest, and reasonable education and living expenses." The ADSO is a minimum of two years and is in addition to the other obligations, such as the three-year ADSO for a direct accession (AR 601-141, 2006). Awards for, say, $40,000 or $80,000 would be paid for one year and two years, respectively, and both awards have an ADSO of two years. An award for $120,000 would be payable for three years and have an ADSO of three years.

Summary

HPSP, FAP, and USUHS all have the potential to cover the costs of medical school, and ADH-PLRP has the potential to pay much of an individual's medical school debt. USUHS does this in-kind and pays at the O-1 level. FAP is in effect a retrospective way of paying for medical school. The FAP award and stipend covers most, and perhaps all, of the cost of one year of medical school, and three or four years of FAP can repay the medical school indebtedness of most medical school graduates. Individuals who went to a public medical school and were in-state residents had lower tuition and could probably pay off their indebtedness with less FAP, as compared with out-of-state students or students who went to a private medical school. HPSP covers the tuition and fees of the medical school one attends and pays a stipend. ADHPLRP provides an incentive for the direct accession of trained, licensed physicians. With an award up to $120,000, it can help cover medical school debt or provide a kitty for opening a private practice after military service.

The programs differ in ADSO. USUHS has a seven-year ADSO while FAP and HPSP have ADSOs up to four years and ADHPLRP has an ADSO of up to three years. USUHS is likely to appeal to individuals with the strongest preference for military service because of the many years of service stemming from it. A four-year HPSP and four-year military residency program involve four-year ADSOs, but they can be served concurrently. HPSP recipients must apply for a military residency and may receive a waiver for a civilian residency. An FAP recipient does not have to apply for a military residency and is typically in a civilian residency. There is a four-year ADSO for three years of FAP.[5] Because HPSP and FAP both cover medical school costs but HPSP may require up to eight years in the military while FAP may require only four, those opting for FAP may have a weaker preference for military service than do HPSP recipients. Similarly, HPSP recipients probably have a weaker preference for military service than do USUHS students. Military preference among ADHPLRP recipients might be like that of FAP recipients, though the maximum FAP ADSO is one year longer than that of ADHPLRP, four years instead of three years. FAP recipients apply for it during their civilian residency, and ADHPLRP recipients apply for it after their residency and possibly after some years of private practice.

HPSP recipients must apply for a military residency, but in psychiatry the chance of being waivered to do a civilian residency may be around 50 percent. HPSP recipients who opt for a civilian residency may have a lower preference for military service than HPSP recipients who do a military residency. But the limited number of military residencies in psychiatry could mean that some individuals who prefer a military residency might have to do a civilian residency instead.

---

[5] A four-year residency has one year of internship and three years afterward. A person applying for FAP must have completed the internship. This person applies for three years of FAP, which has an ADSO of four years.

CHAPTER THREE

Conceptualizing and Modeling the Military Financial Aid Choice and Retention Decision

Trade-Offs in Military Financial Aid

The basic exchange between the individual and the military is money for time—that is, a commitment of military service. The military offers financial aid for a multiyear commitment (ADSO), and the individual accepts the offer to pay for medical school and living expenses.[1] As Chapter Two suggested, the different types of financial aid have differing appeal, depending on the individual's circumstances and taste for military service. This can be described by modeling the financial aid choice, with its military service obligation, in the context of the DRM, and in particular Appendix A presents an expression for the cost to the individual of a two-period commitment relative to a one-period commitment. Here, we discuss the individual's choice of HPSP, FAP, or USUHS, inclusive of the military commitment and relative to the alternative of taking no military financial aid. The choice of ADHPLRP is similar to that of FAP and is not discussed.

Table 3.1 summarizes information about the types of financial aid with respect to the cost of medical school, given that an individual has chosen to go to medical school. Note that the length of residency typically ranges from two to four years, depending on specialty.[2]

As Table 3.1 indicates, FAP and HPSP are geared toward covering the tuition, fees, and living expenses of one year of medical school. HPSP covers the tuition of the medical school one attends. In contrast, FAP pays an annual grant, currently $45,000 per year, which is enough to cover the tuition of most medical schools. HPSP is paid during medical school, while FAP is financial aid to medical school graduates in residency programs. However, the table treats FAP as though it were intended to cover the already-incurred cost of medical school. The inclusion of living expenses in the table is unusual, because they are generally not considered part of a compensation package; living expenses are incurred no matter whether one is working, in school, or out of the labor force. Yet they are relevant to individuals who have made the choice to attend medical school, a full-time activity. Tuition, fees, and living costs represent the amount that must be financed as a student focuses on medical school and

---

[1] One of the major costs of higher education is forgone earnings. So, another way of saying this is that the military stipend (or O-1 compensation) helps to cover the cost of forgone earnings.

[2] Residencies can be several years longer for certain specialties, such as surgery and pathology.

Table 3.1
Military Financial Aid for Psychiatrists

Type	Medical School Cost		Financial Aid					
	Tuition and Fees	Living Expenses	Award	Stipend or Pay[4]	Yearly Difference[5]	Residency Pay	ADSO Years	Years in Military[6]
FAP[1]	T	L	A	$\approx L$	$A - T$	w^n	2 to 5	2 to 5
HPSP, civilian residency[2]	T	L	T	$\approx L$	0	w^n	2 to 4	2 to 4
HPSP, military residency[3]	T	L	T	$\approx L$	0	$w^{m,O\text{-}3}$	3 to 4	7 to 8
USUHS	0	L	0	$w^{m,O\text{-}1}$	$w^{m,O\text{-}1} - L$	$w^{m,O\text{-}3}$	7	11
None	T	L	0	0	$-(T + L)$	w^n	0	0

NOTES: Summary of types of military financial aid available for psychiatrists with respect to the cost of medical school. T = annual tuition, fees, and health insurance cost at the medical school of the individual's choice, given admission; L = annual living expenses, approximately \$25,000 in 2013; A = annual award paid by FAP, \$45,000 in 2013; w^n = annual nonmilitary residency pay, \$50,000–\$56,000 in 2013; $w^{m,O\text{-}1}$ = annual regular military compensation at pay grade O-1, \$53,673 at one year of service, \$63,445 at four years of service for a member with no dependents; $w^{m,O\text{-}3}$ = annual regular military compensation at pay grade O-3, \$72,124 at one year of service, \$87,003 at four years, \$92,971 at eight years with no dependents.

[1] The Army ADSO is one year for each year of participation in FAP, with a minimum of two years, and the Navy and Air Force ADSO is the number of years of FAP participation plus one year, with a minimum of three years. The table assumes that FAP aid is applied against medical school cost.

[2] HPSP has a minimum ADSO of two years, and the ADSO is then one year for each year of participation in HPSP. The HPSP ADSO can be served concurrently with the military residency ADSO.

[3] The residency program in psychiatry is four years. The first year is an internship required for a medical school graduate to be licensed to practice as a physician. A civilian residency does not generate an ADSO. A military residency entails a three-year ADSO.

[4] The FAP and HPSP stipend and summer training pay are approximately equal to annual living expenses during medical school.

[5] The net cost of four years of medical school is approximately $4(T + L) - y(\textit{annual financial aid})$, where y is the number of years of financial aid.

[6] In some cases, e.g., Navy and USUHS, a service member in a military residency program who has completed the internship is given, or elects, an active duty assignment as a GMO. The years in this assignment count against an HPSP ADSO, but they do not count against the seven-year USUHS ADSO. After the GMO assignment, the individual enters a residency program, or, if the HPSP ADSO has been repaid, may leave the military. The GMO assignment increases the number of years in the military by the length of the assignment. The entries in the column assume that there is no GMO assignment.

has no other income.[3] The table omits living expenses when the individual enters a residency program after medical school—as a medical resident, the individual receives a salary.

With no or little income from holding a job while attending medical school, the individual pays tuition, fees, and living expenses by drawing on savings, taking out loans, or receiving financial aid. In the case of FAP and HPSP, the military sets the schedule of aid, and the total amount of aid depends on the number of years of aid. A person with low assets, limited ability to borrow from nonmilitary sources, or unwillingness to incur debt will tend to apply for more years of aid.

---

[3] The cost to be financed is different than the investment cost of attending medical school, which is tuition, fees, and forgone earnings.

The amount of military financial aid sought depends on the taste for military service, military compensation, and career opportunities from military service, relative to compensation, career opportunities, and borrowing constraints in a nonmilitary path. Appendix B incorporates the choice of military financial aid into the DRM framework. An important implication of the analysis is that different financial pathways into the military can influence the distribution of taste for the military at entry. Although our sample of psychiatrists is not large enough to test for fine-grained selectivity, we probe for selectivity when estimating the model by exploring one dimension: Is there evidence of higher taste for military service among USUHS graduates than among HPSP recipients?

Dynamic Retention Model Overview

The DRM is a stochastic dynamic programming model of the decision to stay or leave active duty. It is formulated in terms of the parameters that underlie the retention decision processes and has been described in more detail in previous reports (e.g., Asch, Hosek, and Mattock, 2008; Mattock, Hosek, and Asch, 2012; Asch, Hosek, and Mattock, 2014).

For psychiatrists, the present version of the model begins when the psychiatrist is first observed on active duty at grade O-3. For USUHS graduates or HPSP recipients, this is when they begin their military residency. However, if they obtained a waiver to do a civilian residency, this is the grade at which they enter active duty having completed the civilian residency. For our other occupations, the model begins when they first join active duty. This is typically at grade O-3 for psychologists and O-1 for other occupations (e.g., nurses, occupational therapists, physician assistants, and social workers). In each period, the individual can choose to continue on active duty or to leave active duty. An individual leaving active duty can decide whether to hold only a civilian job, or to hold a civilian job and also to participate in the reserve components. Once having left active duty, the individual cannot return to it, but can move back and forth between the reserve and civilian states.

We denote the value of staying in the active component at time t as

$$V_t^S = V_t^A + \varepsilon_t^A,$$

where V_t^A is the nonstochastic value of the active alternative and ε_t^A is a random shock.

The value of leaving at time t is

$$V_t^L = max[V_t^R + \omega_t^R, V_t^C + \omega_t^C] + \varepsilon_t^L,$$

where the member can choose between reserve and civilian. "Civilian" means working at a nonmilitary job, and "reserve" means participating in a reserve component and working at a nonmilitary job. The value of reserve is given by $V_t^R + \omega_t^R$, while value of civilian is given by $V_t^C + \omega_t^C$. We model the reserve/civilian choice as a nest and will assume that the stochastic terms follow an extreme value distribution, which leads to a nested logit specification.[4] The within-nest shocks to the reserve/civilian choice are given by ω_t^R and ω_t^C, while the nest-specific shock is given by ε_t^L.

---

[4] See Train (2009) for a discussion of the logit and nested logit specifications.

The shock terms represent a variety of events, such as a good assignment, dangerous mission, strong civilian job market, opportunity for promotion, new location, change in marital status, change in dependency status, change in health status, or the prospect of deployment or deployment itself. We allow a common shock across the reserve and civilian nest, ϵ_T^L, since an individual in the reserves also holds a civilian job, as well as shock terms specific to the reserve and civilian states, ω_t^R and ω_t^C. The individual is assumed to know the distributions that generate the shocks and the shock realizations in the current period but not in future periods. The distributions are assumed constant over time, and the shocks are uncorrelated within and between periods. Once a future period is reached and the shocks are realized, the individual can re-optimize, i.e., choose the alternative with the maximum value at that time. But in the current period, the future realizations are not known, so the individual assesses the future period by taking the expected value of the maximum. For instance, depending on the shocks as well compensation, there is some chance that V_t^S will be greater than V_t^L, in which case V_t^S would be the maximum, and vice versa, and the individual makes an assessment of the expected value of the maximum, $Emax(V_t^S, V_t^L)$.

We assume that the shocks have extreme value distributions and, as mentioned, the civilian and reserve choice is nested. The extreme value distribution, denoted EV, has location parameter a and scale parameter b; the mean is $b\phi$ and the variance is $\pi^2 b^2/6$, where ϕ is Euler's gamma (~0.577). As we derive in past studies, this implies

$$\varepsilon_t^A \sim EV\left[-\phi\sqrt{\lambda^2 + \tau^2}, \sqrt{\lambda^2 + \tau^2}\right]$$

$$\omega_t^T \sim EV[-\phi\lambda, \lambda]$$

$$\omega_t^C \sim EV[-\phi\lambda, \lambda]$$

$$\varepsilon_t^L \sim EV[-\phi\tau, \tau]$$

where λ is the scale parameter of the distribution of ω_t^R and ω_t^C and τ is the scale parameter of the distribution of ε_t^L. Because of the nesting structure of the model, this implies that the scale parameter of ε_t^A can be written as $\sqrt{\lambda^2 + \tau^2}$. For convenience, we define $\kappa = \sqrt{\lambda^2 + \tau^2}$ and refer to it as the scale parameter for the total error. Similarly, the scale parameter of ε_t^L can be written as $\sqrt{\lambda^1 + \tau^1}$. To put the outcomes on the same scale, we impose $\kappa = \sqrt{\lambda^1 + \tau^1} = \sqrt{\lambda^2 + \tau^2}$.

The symbols of the model are summarized in Table 6.1.

The values of the alternatives V_t^A, V_t^R, and V_t^C depend on the current-period pay associated with serving in an active component or working as a civilian, W_t^a or W_t^c. If the individual is a reservist, he or she earns the civilian wage plus reserve pay, $W_t^c + W_t^r$. In addition, each individual has tastes for active and reserve duty, γ_a and γ_r, respectively, which also enter the value functions for active and reserve. Each taste represents the individual's perceived net advantage of holding an active or reserve position, relative to the civilian state. Other things equal, a higher taste for active or reserve service increases retention. The tastes are assumed to be constant over time but may vary across individuals. The tastes are not observed but are assumed to follow a bivariate normal distribution over active component entrants.

The nonstochastic part of the value of staying active, V_t^A, can therefore be written as

$$V_t^A = \gamma_a + W_t^a + \beta E\left[max[V_{t+1}^L, V_{t+1}^S] \right],$$

where β is the personal discount factor.

The possibility of re-optimizing in future periods is a key feature of dynamic programming models that distinguishes them from other dynamic models. Re-optimization means that the individual can choose the best alternative in a period when its conditions have been realized, i.e., when the shocks are known. In the current period, with future realizations unknown, the best the individual can do is estimate the expected value of the best choice in the next period, i.e., the expected value of the maximum. Logically, this will also be true in the following period, and the one after it, and so forth, so the model is forward-looking and rationally handles future uncertainty. Thus, today's decision takes into account the possibility of future changes of state and assumes that future decisions will also be optimizing.

The nonstochastic values of the reserve choice and civilian choice can be written as

$$V_t^R = \gamma_r + W_t^c + W_t^r + \beta E\left[max[V_{t+1}^R + \omega_r, V_{t+1}^C + \omega_c] \right]$$

$$V_t^C = W_t^c + R_t + \beta E\left[max[V_{t+1}^R + \omega_r, V_{t+1}^C + \omega_c] \right]$$

where R_t in the civilian equation is the present value of any active or reserve military retirement benefit for which the individual is eligible.

The model has three switching costs. These costs are not actually paid by the individual but are implicit in making certain transitions. The first is a cost of leaving active duty before ADSO is completed. The second is a cost of not participating in active or reserve service before the total service obligation is completed. The third is a cost of switching into the reserve from the civilian state. This cost could represent difficulty in finding an available reserve position in a desired geographic location or a possible negative impact on one's civilian job, e.g., from not being available to work on certain weekends or for two weeks in the summer or being subject to reserve call-up.

Although the individual does not know when future military promotions will occur, we assume that the individual knows the promotion policy and pay scales and forms an expectation of military pay in future periods. Similarly, the individual forms an expectation of civilian pay.

Extending the DRM to Handle Multiyear Special Pay

The main innovation to the DRM in this report, compared with our earlier studies, is incorporating the choice of MSP obligation into the DRM for psychiatrists. MSP is available after completion of the initial ADSO and entails a two-, three-, or four-year obligation; the individual chooses the length of obligation. Incentive Special Play (ISP), which may be more generous when members also take MSP (though in the case of psychiatrists there is no interaction between ISP and MSP amounts), involves a one-year obligation. For psychiatrists, we expanded the structure of the DRM to allow members to make an ISP/MSP decision with its accompanying service obligation. The methodology follows Mattock and Arkes (2007), which models the five-year and 20-year commitment associated with Aviator Continuation Pay (ACP) for Air Force rated officers. Unlike Mattock and Arkes, the DRM here includes the opportunity to participate in the reserve components, and, of course, the structure of MSP differs from that of ACP.

The other mental health care occupations began to be eligible for S&I pays that involve a choice of a service obligation only after 2010 and thus after the period covered by our data. Consequently, for psychiatrists, we incorporate the MSP choice into both the estimation computer code and into the simulation code. For the other mental health care providers, we incorporate the S&I pay/obligation choice into our simulation code but not the estimation code. Here, we present the mathematical expressions for including the choice of MSP/obligation. The expressions generalize to other pays that involve a service obligation choice.

We include the MSP choice by adding equations that express the value of the MSP program for different obligation lengths. The DRM described above involves two equations. The first is the value of staying active, and the second is the value of leaving, which is a nest of the reserve and civilian choice. Because our focus is on the multiyear choice while a member is on active duty, we ignore the nest and describe the value of leaving simply as V_t^L.

The equation V_t^S gives the value of staying active for one additional year, at time t. Thus, we can write the value of staying active for one more year as

$$V_t^{S|1} = V_t^{A|1} + \varepsilon_t^A = \gamma_a + W_t^a + \beta E\left[max[V_{t+1}^L, V_{t+1}^S]\right] + \varepsilon_t^A ,$$

where W_t^a now includes ISP.

We can write the value of staying active and taking the MSP with a two-year obligation as

$$V_t^{S|2} = V_t^{A|2} + \varepsilon_t^A = \sum_{n=0}^{1} \beta^n[\gamma_a + W_t^a] + \beta^k E\left[max[V_{t+k}^L, V_{t+k}^S]\right] + \varepsilon_t^A .$$

The errors in the intervening periods covered by the commitment are inconsequential because there is no stay/leave choice to be made and the expected value of the error in each period is zero. In contrast, in a future period when a choice can be made, the better alternative will be chosen, and it is evaluated in the current period as the expected value of the maximum of that future choice.

Similarly, the value staying active and taking MSP with a k-year obligation is

$$V_t^{S|k} = V_t^{A|k} + \varepsilon_t^A = \sum_{n=0}^{k-1} \beta^n[\gamma_a + W_t^a] + \beta^k E\left[max[V_{t+k}^L, V_{t+k}^S]\right] + \varepsilon_t^A .$$

An eligible psychiatrist compares the value of leaving, V_t^L, with the maximum of the value of staying for one year, $V_t^{S|1}$; two years, $V_t^{S|2}$; or k years, where k can be as high as four years in the case of MSP. The probability that an initially offered psychiatrist will stay active is

$$\Pr\left(max\left[V_t^{S|1}, V_t^{S|2}, V_t^{S|3}, V_t^{S|4} \right] > V^L \right).$$

Like the reserve/civilian choice, the MSP obligation choice can be handled as a nested choice. If we assume the random shocks of the MSP obligation choice follow an extreme value distribution, we can write $\varepsilon_t^{A|k} \sim EV[-\phi\lambda_2, \lambda_2]$, where λ_2 is the scale parameter and is subscripted with 2 to distinguish is from the shape parameter for the within-reserve/civilian nest shock, defined above, which we now denote as λ_1, e.g., $\omega_t^R \sim EV[-\phi\lambda_1, \lambda_1]$. Thus, the MSP choice adds another parameter to be estimated.

Information Necessary to Implement the Mental Health Professional DRMs

DRM estimation requires three types of data. These are individual-level longitudinal data on active retention and subsequent participation, if any, in the reserve components, and expected military and civilian pay over a career. Chapters Four and Five develop estimates of expected military and civilian pay, and Chapter Six describes the longitudinal retention data. Chapter Six also discusses the estimation methodology, parameter estimates, and model fits.

CHAPTER FOUR

Active Component Earnings of Mental Health Professionals

This chapter discusses the active duty earnings of psychiatrists, psychologists, and other mental health professionals. We describe basic pay and RMC, the tables for which are common across all officer occupations. We discuss the expected military earnings of psychiatrists, also describing our approach. As a sidelight, we compare the military earnings of psychiatrists with the military earnings of other specialties, and Chapter Five shows the civilian earnings of physicians by specialty. We then present military earnings for psychologists, nurses, occupational therapists, physician assistants, and social workers. Our chief sources are the 2009 tables for basic pay, allowances, and S&I pays. The DRM also requires reserve pay, and Appendix C describes our approach to calculating it.

Basic Pay and Regular Military Compensation by Years of Service

We calculated the average basic pay by YOS for each occupation. We used the 2009 basic pay tables and constructed a weighed average of basic pay by YOS, where the weights were the proportion of officers in that occupation by grade at that YOS. We use grades to O-7,[1] and for psychiatrists and psychologists we begin at O-3 (the grade when starting residency). We took the same approach for RMC. RMC includes basic pay, basic allowance for housing (BAH), basic allowance for subsistence (BAS), and a federal income tax advantage due to the nontaxability of the allowances.

Special and Incentive Pay for Psychiatrists

Psychiatrists on active duty are eligible for a number of S&I pays. There are various rationales for these pays, including "extraordinarily high civilian earnings opportunities," "high training/replacement costs," "rapid demand growth," "onerous or dangerous conditions of service," "special skills and proficiency," and "performance or productivity" (Hogan et al., 2012). In 1980, the Uniformed Services Health Professionals Special Pay Act established four types of special pays for physicians: Variable Special Pay (VSP), Additional Special Pay (ASP), Board Certified Pay (BCP), and ISP. A Medical Officer Retention Bonus was created in 1989 but replaced in 1991 by the Multiyear Retention Bonus, also known as Multiyear Special Pay (MSP) (U.S. Department of Defense, Office of the Under Secretary of Defense for Personnel

---

[1] There were no health service officers above grade O-7 in the 2009 DMDC data.

and Readiness, 2005). Nearly all physicians receive VSP and ASP, and once they are board-certified they also receive BCP. MSP is offered at the discretion of the Secretary of Defense, who "may decline to offer MSP to any specialty that is otherwise eligible or restrict the length of an MSP contract for a specialty to less than 4 years" (U.S. Department of Defense, 2008). In practice, this means that MSP offers can be tailored by specialty.

VSP, ASP, and BCP have remained the same since 1991. VSP is available to any physician on active duty for one year and is payable monthly. All physicians, including residents, are eligible for VSP. The amount varies by the number of years of creditable service and ranges from $1,500 per year to $12,000 per year, and is $1,200 for residents. ASP is available to physicians who have completed their initial residency. ASP is payable yearly, and accepting ASP requires a commitment to serve through the current year. ASP is $15,000 and is paid at the beginning of the year. Any "unearned" portion must be refunded if the physician leaves before the year is completed. BCP is available to physicians who are eligible for VSP and have passed their board certification exam. The amount varies by years of creditable service and ranges from $2,500 to $6,000 per year (U.S. Department of Defense, 2008).

ISP and MSP are for physicians who have completed their ADSO. Unlike VSP, ASP, and BCP, the maximum amounts of ISP and MSP have changed over time and vary by specialty. The amount of ISP may differ depending on whether a physician also signs an MSP contract, though in the case of psychiatrists there is no interaction between ISP and MSP amounts.

Table 4.1 shows the S&I pay amounts for psychiatrists in years 2000 and 2009, in then-year dollars. VSP, ASP, and BCP were constant, but ISP and MSP increased. In FY 2009, ISP without MSP ranged from $20,000 to $36,000, while ISP with MSP ranged from $20,000 to $41,000, depending on the specialty. MSP was $12,000 to $25,000 per year for a two-year contract, $13,000 to $40,000 per year for a three-year contract, and $20,000 to $60,000 per year for a four-year contract. For psychiatrists, ISP was $20,000 in FY 2009 regardless of whether the psychiatrist signed an MSP contract, while MSP was $17,000 per year for a two-year contract, $28,000 per year for a three-year contract, and $43,000 per year for a four-year contract. In FY 2000, psychiatrist ISP was $14,000 and MSP was $9,000, $10,000, and $14,000 per year for two-, three-, and four-year contracts, respectively.

Figure 4.1 displays psychiatrist S&I pay from FY 1993 to FY 2015 in 2009 dollars for a psychiatrist with ten to 12 years of service. Total S&I pay was roughly constant from 1993 to 2006. The total increased from FY 2006 to FY 2009, the peak year, then declined because of erosion from inflation. The increase from FY 2006 to FY 2009 came from increases in ISP and MSP, and there were large increases in MSP for three- and especially four-year contracts. Much of these increases came in the years immediately following the press coverage, starting in February 2007, of lack of services and care for veterans at Walter Reed Army Medical Center and the need to care for the growing number of service members with posttraumatic stress disorder (PTSD) and depression.

Defense Manpower Data Center (DMDC) pay files are available from 1993 onward and allow us to see what percentage of psychiatrists received S&I pays (Figure 4.2). The figure is limited to those who did their residency in the military.[2] It shows the percentage of psychiatrists in the 1990–2000 cohorts receiving each type of S&I pay by YOS. The percentage

---

[2] Among the 417 psychiatrists in the 1990–2000 cohorts, 267 appear to have entered through HPSP and 53 through USUHS. 220 of the HPSPs went on to a military residency, and another 34 appear to have completed a civilian residency while serving in the reserves. Nearly all USUHS students (50 out of 53) went on to a military residency. Of the remain-

Table 4.1
Special and Incentive Pays Available to Psychiatrists, 2000 and 2009

Special or Incentive Pay	Requirements	Annual Amount for Psychiatrists in 2009 (2009$)	Annual Amount for Psychiatrists in 2000 (2000$)
Variable Special Pay	Available to all physicians.	$5,000 to $12,000 depending on YOS ($1,200 for internship)	$5,000 to $12,000 depending on YOS ($1,200 for internship)
Additional Special Pay	Available to all physicians not on internship or residency.	$15,000	$15,000
Board Certified Pay	Available to board-certified physicians.	$2,500 to $6,000 depending on years of creditable service	$2,500 to $6,000 depending on years of creditable service
Incentive Special Pay	Available to physicians below grade O-7 who have completed their specialty qualifications. Requires a one-year contract.	$20,000	$14,000
Multiyear Special Pay	Available to physicians below grade O-7 with 8 or more years of creditable service or those who have completed service obligation. Requires a two-, three-, or four-year contract.	$17,000/year (2 years) $28,000/year (3 years) $43,000/year (4 years)	$9,000/year (2 years) $10,000/year (3 years) $14,000/year (4 years)

SOURCES: Summary of S&I pays available for psychiatrists in 2000 and 2009, based on U.S. Department of Defense (1999, 2008).

Figure 4.1
S&I Pay for a Psychiatrist with 10–12 Years of Service (2009 $)

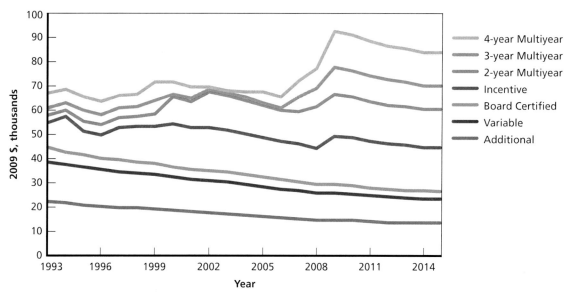

SOURCE: Defense Finance and Accounting Service, 2016.
NOTE: Summary of S&I pay amounts available for psychiatrists.
RAND RR1425-4.1

ing psychiatrists, 34 were initially observed on active duty as residents, and were thus likely accessed through FAP, while another 61 appear to be direct accessions.

Figure 4.2
Percentage of Psychiatrists Receiving Special and Incentive Pays by Years of Active Duty Service, 1990–2000 Cohorts: Military Residents

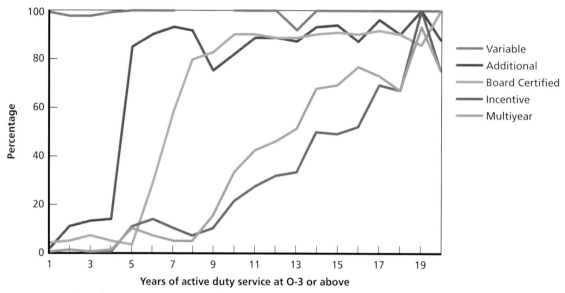

SOURCE: Based on the 1990–2000 cohorts of active duty psychiatrists observed in the DMDC pay files.
NOTE: Percentage of active duty psychiatrists observed receiving each type of S&I pay, by years of active duty service at O-3 or above.
RAND RR1425-4.2

is the average over the 1990 to 2000 cohorts. The YOS count begins when an officer is first observed as an O-3 or above, which indicates the start of the residency. As expected, nearly all psychiatrists receive VSP.[3] ASP is available after a psychiatrist completes residency. Consistent with a four-year residency, ASP receipt increases sharply in YOS 5. It nearly reaches 95 percent in years 6 and 7, then falls to around 80–90 percent. The decrease may reflect hesitancy to commit to another year in the military when some psychiatrists may be prospecting for civilian jobs. When we do not limit the figure to those who did their residency in the military, ASP receipt is 10–20 percent in YOS 2 to 4. We think this occurs because some HPSP recipients did a civilian residency and had completed it when they entered active duty, making them eligible for ASP. BCP also picks up in YOS 6, when psychiatrists start becoming certified. ISP and MSP receipt increases after YOS 8, when most psychiatrists have completed their ADSO.

Based on policy and actual receipt of S&I pays (Figure 4.2), in building a military pay line—that is, expected military pay by YOS—we assumed that all eligible psychiatrists would receive VSP, ASP, and BCP. For ISP, we assumed that a psychiatrist looking ahead to future stay-leave decisions would take into account the probability of receiving it. We multiplied the published value of ISP in 2009 by the fraction of psychiatrists actually receiving the pay, by YOS, based on the pay files. Using the percentage that receives S&I pay times the median value is behaviorally equivalent to agents assuming random assignment of that pay (i.e., they cannot influence it). Alternatively, it is equivalent to assuming that an individual uses the population

---

[3] The DMDC pay files at RAND appear to be missing information about VSP from 1997 through 2008. Therefore, there are gaps in our analysis of VSP.

average to predict the individual's expected pay in the future.[4] For MSP, we created DRM code to allow the individual to choose either the two-, three-, or four-year commitment.

Figure 4.3 shows a psychiatrist's expected earnings over a military career assuming a three-year MSP multiplied by the fraction of psychiatrists observed receiving MSP by YOS and using the 2009 pay tables. As discussed, the most common path to becoming a military physician is through HPSP and a military residency. The figure assumes that the psychiatrist spends four years on HPSP in medical school followed by a four-year military residency.

The horizontal axis of Figure 4.3 shows YOS starting when the psychiatrist graduates from medical school and begins his or her military residency. During the four-year residency, the psychiatrist is eligible only for VSP. In the next four years (YOS 5 through 8), the psychiatrist has completed his or her residency and is paying off his or her ADSO. The psychiatrist is eligible for ASP in addition to VSP and could qualify for BCP. After ADSO (YOS 9 and above), the psychiatrist is also eligible for ISP and MSP. Total pay increases from $71,000 in YOS 1 to $186,000 in YOS 20. The somewhat jagged nature of expected pay comes from year-to-year variation in the percentage of psychiatrists receiving a special pay (Figure 4.2).

Figure 4.3 does not include the Accession Bonus for Critically Short Wartime Specialties. This bonus is available to physicians in certain specialties but only to those who had not received any financial assistance to study medicine. An HPSP recipient would not be eligible, for instance. In FY 2011, the bonus was capped at $272,000 for psychiatrists joining the Army (U.S. Army Recruiting Command, 2010) and paid annually over four years.

Figure 4.3
Basic Pay, RMC, and Total Pay Including Various Special Pays for Psychiatrists by Years of Active Duty Service According to 2009 Pay Table

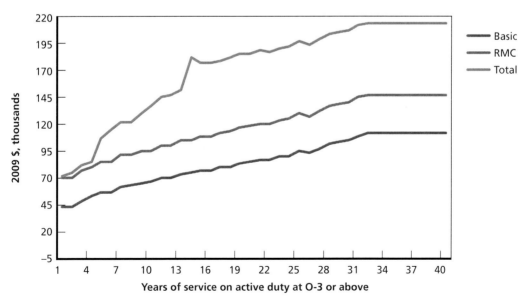

SOURCES: Estimated average values of basic pay, RMC, and total pay (including S&I pay) for psychiatrists, based on the 2009 pay table, U.S. Department of Defense (2008), and DMDC pay files.
RAND RR1425-4.3

---

[4] Also, the linearity of the DRM implies that the variance of the value of S&I pay, conditional on receipt, is not relevant. As a result, we do not need the variance of S&I as an input to the DRM.

Also not included is Early Career Incentive Special Pay (ECISP) for physicians who have completed their residency and are within 18 months of completing their ADSO. ECISP for psychiatrists is currently $39,000 per year for a four-year contractual obligation in 2009. When an ECSIP recipient has completed ADSO, he or she can recontract for MSP, that is, terminate ECISP by entering into an MSP contract with a longer obligation. We do not include ECISP because it was created after 2009 and was not available to cohorts in our data.

We also examined the extent to which our military pay line was similar to the actual pay of our cohorts using DMDC active duty pay files from 1993 to 2009. This analysis, shown in Appendix D, finds that actual pay increased faster than our pay line. As discussed in the appendix, the faster increase reflects the rapid growth in real military pay in the past decade, a trend that has not continued.

Active Duty Pay by Physician Specialty

Figure 4.4 shows median total active duty pay across physician specialties. The figure is based on the 2009 pay files for Army physicians. We included only those who received ASP; this serves to limit the sample to physicians who have completed their residency. We used Army physician data because occupation codes are easiest to identify in this service.

Not surprisingly, the ranking of occupations by military pay can differ from the ranking by civilian pay shown in Chapter Five. Various surgical specialties and internal medicine sub-specialties are near the top of both distributions, and internal medicine and pediatrics are near the bottom. Anesthesiology is near the bottom of the military pay scale though near the top of the civilian pay scale. Occupational medicine, infectious medicine, and preventive medicine are near the top of the military scale but are lower in the civilian pay scale. In both military and civilian pay scales, psychiatrists fall in the lower-middle part of the distribution.

In three-fourths of the specialties, median military pay is in the range of $110,000 to $160,000 per year, and one-fourth of the specialties have pay of $160,000 to $200,000 per year. The median pay of psychiatrists was $126,788 and lies about a third of the way up the distribution.

Figure 4.5 shows total pay by YOS for the larger specialties in Figure 4.4. The pay range across specialties is fairly narrow, e.g., about $10,000 at YOS 4 to 8 and $15,000 at YOS 9 to 15. The range appears to widen in higher years. But this occurs because these more-senior personnel benefited from the higher-than-usual pay increases in the past decade, including the boost in MSP from 2007 to 2009 (Appendix D, Figure D.1).

Special and Incentive Pay for Psychologists

Like physicians, psychologists have a variety of career paths in joining the military, including HPSP, USUHS, and joining directly.[5] Most psychologists in our data set appear to be direct accessions and were first observed at grade O-3. Direct accession as a psychologist has a three-

---

[5] Eligibility for FAP requires the individual to be a medical school graduate. We assume most psychologists have not graduated from medical school.

Figure 4.4
Median Total Pay Among Army Nonresidents, by Specialty, 2009 (2009 $)

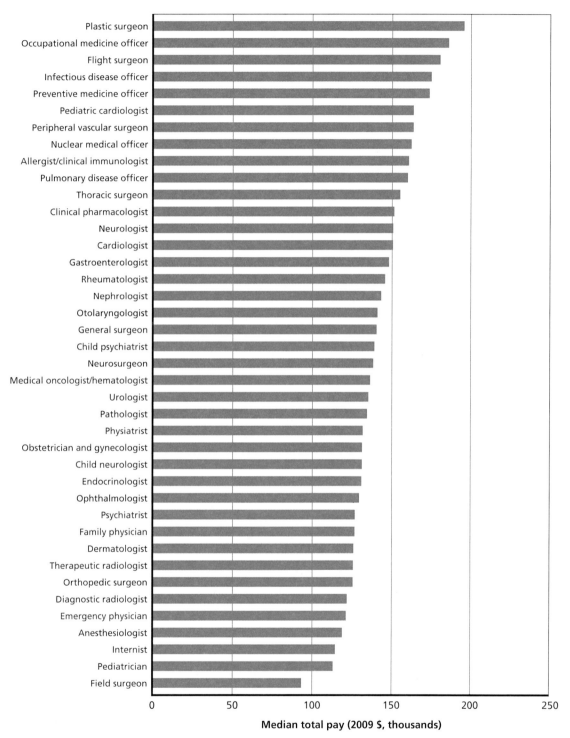

SOURCE: Estimated median values of total pay for medical Army officers from the 1990–2000 cohorts who were not identified as medical residents, by specialty, based on DMDC pay files.
RAND *RR1425-4.4*

Figure 4.5
Median Physician Compensation by Years of Active Duty Service and Specialty,
1990–2000 Cohorts (2009 $)

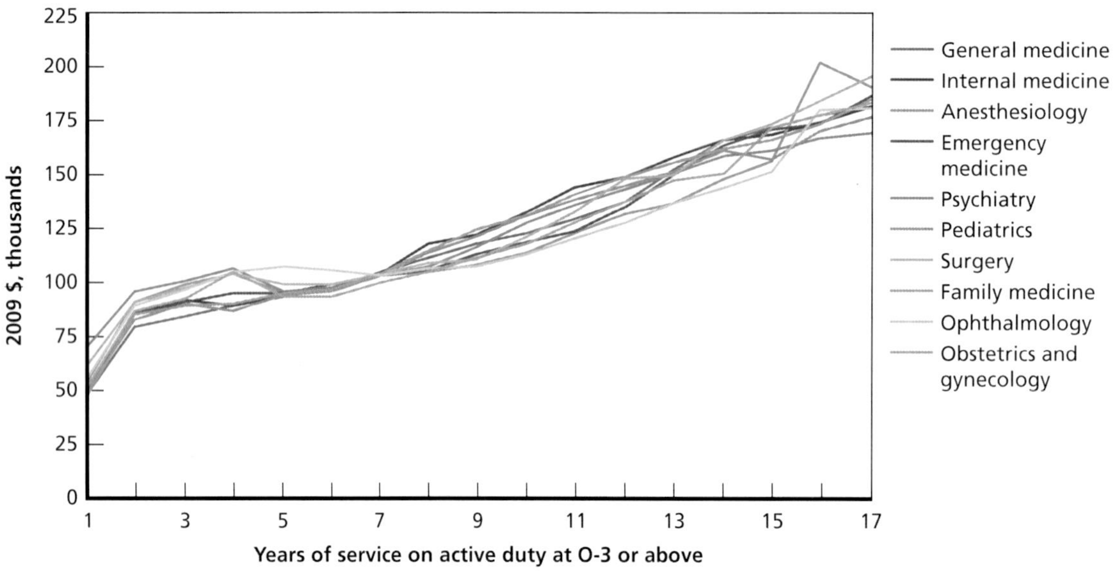

SOURCE: Estimated median values of total pay for medical Army officers from the 1990–2000 cohorts who were not identified as residents, by specialty and years of service, based on DMDC pay files.
RAND *RR1425-4.5*

year minimum service obligation.[6] Few psychologists appear to have participated in USUHS or HPSP. Among the 515 psychologists we studied, none were flagged as having studied at USUHS. We identified 42 psychologists as likely HPSP recipients based on time spent on reserve duty at grade O-1. Receiving funds from HPSP incurs a one-year obligation for every year of funding, with a two-year minimum in the Army and three-year minimum in the Navy and Air Force. Psychologists must complete a one- or two-year internship following the completion of a Ph.D. program. We assumed that psychologists who entered the military through HPSP had completed a military internship and that ADSO payback began after this time.

We calculated the average basic pay and RMC received by psychologists starting when they first reached grade O-3 or above and were classified as a psychologist, using the same pay-table approach we used for psychiatrists. The 2009 pay tables were used, and calculated pay is in 2009 dollars.

Psychologists in our cohorts were eligible for Diplomate Pay ranging from $2,000 to $5,000 per year depending on YOS (Table 4.2).

Figure 4.6 shows psychologist pay, including the Diplomate Pay. Total pay at the first year of O-3 is about $72,000. It is $97,000 at YOS 10 and $123,000 at YOS 20.

---

[6] Direct accessions may be eligible for ADHPLRP, which incurs an additional obligation (Chapter Two).

Table 4.2
Diplomate Pay/Board Certified Pay

YOS	Amount
<10	$2,000
10–12	$2,500
12–14	$3,000
14–18	$4,000
18+	$5,000

SOURCE: Amount of Diplomate Pay/BCP
available for psychologists, by YOS, based
on U.S. Department of Defense (2008).

Figure 4.6
Basic Pay, RMC, and Total Pay Including Special Pay for Psychologists by Years of Active Duty Service According to 2009 Pay Table

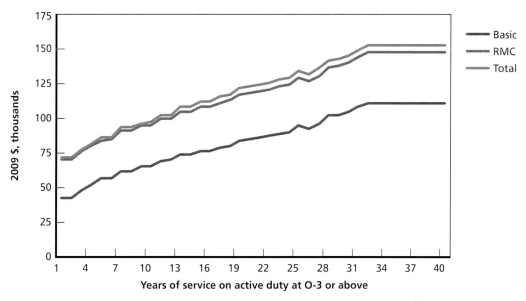

SOURCES: Estimated average values of basic pay, RMC, and total pay for psychologists, based on the
2009 pay table and on U.S. Department of Defense (2008).
RAND RR1425-4.6

Special and Incentive Pay for Other Mental Health Professionals

These include registered nurses, occupational therapists, physician assistants, and social workers. A military career in nursing typically requires a registered nurse certification, usually obtained after a bachelor's degree in nursing. The other occupations typically require one to two years of training after a bachelor's degree.

We analyzed cohorts who were first observed on active duty in one of these occupations between 1990 and 2000. We considered all officers in these occupations, not specifically mental health providers, because the occupational codes available in the data typically did not allow us to identify whether the individual's duties related to mental health. In one occupation, nursing, we were able to identify a subset of nurses who performed mental health–related duties at some point during their military careers.

Nearly all officers in these occupations were first observed at grade O-1 and appear to be direct accessions. Direct accessions have a three-year minimum service obligation. A few of the nurses attended USUHS, and a few additional nurses, as well as physician assistants, participated in the HPSP program based on their time served on O-1 reserve duty. Other nurses may have attended non-USUHS programs offered by the military, but we were unable to identify which, if any, nurses in our cohorts attended these programs. These programs are typically two to four years long and have an ADSO of four to five years.

We calculated military pay for officers in these occupations starting when we first observed them on active duty in that occupation, using a similar methodology as for psychiatrists and psychologists though including O-1 and O-2. Like psychologists, other health service providers were eligible for Diplomate Pay/BCP ranging from $2,000 to $5,000 per year, depending on YOS during the time period we examined (Table 4.2).

Some nurses in the DMDC pay files received pay classified as a bonus. Forty percent of nurses at YOS 1 were observed receiving this bonus, suggesting that it was linked to accession. Beyond YOS 1, 1 to 10 percent of nurses received a bonus. The median bonus was $5,000 among recipients. We treated the bonus like we treated ISP and MSP for psychiatrists, adding in the expected value of the bonus computed as the fraction of nurses receiving it multiplied by the median amount. We applied the BCP to all occupations, and the expected value of the nurse bonus to nurses. We found that the total pay line for nurses is essentially identical to that for the "other" category, which includes occupational therapists, physician assistants, and social workers (Figure 4.7).

Figure 4.7
Basic Pay, RMC, and Total Pay Including Special Pay for Other Mental Health Providers by Years of Active Duty Service According to 2009 Pay Table

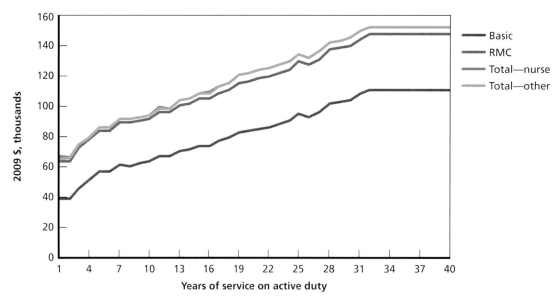

SOURCES: Estimated average values of basic pay, RMC, and total pay for nurses and other mental health providers, based on the 2009 pay table, U.S. Department of Defense (2008), and the DMDC pay files.
RAND RR1425-4.7

We also calculated basic pay, RMC, and total pay for the 1990–2000 cohorts of each of these occupations, using the active duty pay files (Appendix D). We find that the actual pay line is somewhat lower than the published 2009 pay line for each YOS, again likely due to the rise in the real value of basic pay in the past decade.

Summary

We computed expected military pay by year of service for psychiatrists, psychologists, nurses, occupational therapists, physician assistants, and social workers using the 2009 tables for basic pay and housing and subsistence allowances and relevant S&I pays. Where all or nearly all received an S&I pay, we applied it in full, and where only a fraction received the pay we applied its expected value, computed as the percentage receiving the pay times the median value of the pay among recipients. The underlying assumption is that individuals base their pay expectation on the population average. We also include MSP, and for this the DRM allows the individual to choose the length of obligation. That is, our empirical approach allows the contract length to be endogenous (a choice of the individual). Because our civilian pay profiles—another input to the DRM—are in 2013 dollars, as we describe in the next chapter, we put the expected military pay profiles in 2013 dollars as well using the Consumer Price Index for urban consumers.

We compared the expected pay lines we developed with those computed directly from military pay for the cohorts in our sample, finding that the latter increase more rapidly from YOS 1 to 20 than did the pay lines we developed. This comes from the relatively rapid growth of inflation-adjusted military pay in the past decade, which is not expected to continue.

We tabulated median total pay for Army physician specialties and found psychiatrist pay of $126,788 in 2009 (2009 dollars) to be about a third of the way up the pay distribution.

CHAPTER FIVE

Civilian Earnings of Mental Health Professionals

This chapter discusses the earnings of civilian physicians, psychologists, nurses, occupational therapists, physician assistants, and social workers. We estimate earnings regressions for full-time, full-year workers in these occupations and use the results to predict expected earnings by age, which are needed for estimating the DRM. Figures in this chapter show predicted earnings for the 40th through 90th deciles of earnings by age, based on the American Community Survey (ACS) regression results. We briefly discuss male/female differences in physician earnings and the earnings of medical residents and fellows.

Our main data come from the ACS for years 2003 through 2012 (U.S. Census Bureau, no date-a). The ACS asks about earnings in the previous year, so the earnings are for 2002 through 2011. ACS occupation coding identifies psychologists, nurses, occupational therapists, physician assistants, and social workers, but psychiatrists are grouped with physicians in general. We address this limitation by referencing other data on physician earnings by specialty. These data indicate that psychiatrist earnings are approximately equal to median physician earnings.

The other data are from the Bureau of Labor Statistics Occupational Employment Statistics Survey (OES; Bureau of Labor Statistics, no date-c)[1] and from the American Medical Group Association (AMGA; American Medical Group Association, 2011). The OES has income by specialty but does not have covariates, such as age and education, or data at the individual level. AMGA data have median physician earnings for many specialties but only for group practices, most of which are large. Even so, AMGA data are a useful source of earnings because younger physicians increasingly join group practices. We also considered Medscape survey data.[2]

American Community Survey Data

We selected ACS data on individuals with four or more years of college, 40 or more usual weekly hours of work, and 50–52 weeks of work in one year—full-time, full-year, college-

---

[1] The OES focuses on employment by occupation and is conducted by the Bureau of Labor Statistics. The OES brings in wage information from the National Compensation Survey (NCS; Bureau of Labor Statistics, no date-b). The OES has a larger number of occupations than NCS, while NCS makes finer distinctions than OES with regard to the duties and responsibilities of the job within an occupation. Both OES and NCS cover the same eight physician specialties, and OES earnings estimates incorporate NCS wage information. For our purposes, OES subsumes NCS.

[2] Medscape employs contractors to conduct its online surveys, but the representativeness of the surveys is unclear. This makes us reluctant to use the Medscape data.

educated workers. We adjusted earnings are adjusted to 2013 dollars by the Consumer Price Index for All Urban Consumers.

ACS income-related data are top-coded. Amounts above a threshold are not reported, although a flag indicates top coding. The threshold varies by state. To control for top-coding, we estimate right-censored Tobit regressions. For top-coded earnings, the Tobit likelihood includes an expression for probability of earnings being above the threshold, and for non-top-coded earnings, the likelihood includes an expression for the probability of the exact value of the earnings. Not controlling for top-coding risks biasing the regression line, such that the increase in earnings with age would be shallower than actual.

The ACS is a cross-sectional survey, and our ACS surveys form a sample of pooled cross-sections. The regression estimates and predictions based on them describe the wage-age relationship in the cross-section.[3] We assume that individuals base their earnings expectations by age on the earnings of workers currently at that age.

Methods

The earnings regression specification is log-linear and assumes that the error of log earnings is normally distributed as

$$\ln(Earnings) = \beta_0 + \beta_1 Age + \beta_2 Age^2 + \beta_3 Female +$$
$$\beta_4 More\ than\ 4\ years\ of\ college + \beta_5 Veteran +$$
$$\beta_6 Veteran\ 1990\ to\ 2001 + \beta_7 Veteran\ 2001\ to\ 2011 +$$
$$\sum_{2003}^{2011} \delta_t + \sum_{2}^{7} \delta_q + \varepsilon$$

The natural log of earnings is a function of age, age-squared, gender, education level, veteran status, year fixed effects, top-code threshold level indicators, and an error term. There are three veteran indicators: veteran, veteran serving in 1990 to 2001, and veteran serving in 2001 to 2012. Age represents years of experience, although with some error. Years of experience depend on the age when education is completed and work in the profession begins. This varies by health profession, by whether there are breaks in education, and by whether education is done on a part-time basis. With full-time education and no breaks, experience approximately equals age minus years of education minus six. In this case, age accurately represents experience, assuming the required years of education in a profession are fixed. Still, health profession curricula typically have clinical hours requirements, and these hours might be countable as experience even though education is still underway. Overall, because age imperfectly controls for experience, the estimated increase in earnings with age might be shallower than if we had experience. A "veteran" is a person who served on active duty in the past but not at the time of the survey. "Veteran 1990 to 2001" indicates that the most recent period of service was

---

[3] In work not reported here, we found that earnings curves based on synthetic cohorts were very similar to earnings curves predicted from cross-sections. A synthetic cohort assembles earnings for, say, workers age 25 to 30 in 1995, 30 to 35 in 2000, 35 to 40 in 2005, etc.

between 1990 and 2001, and "veteran 2001 to 2012" indicates that the most recent period of service was in or after 2001 to 2012.

The year and threshold indicators, δ_t and δ_q, capture year fixed effects, such as the state of the economy, and guard against the possibility that higher-earning workers tend to live in states with higher thresholds. If the threshold fixed effects were not included, a correlation between the threshold and the other explanatory variables could bias their estimated coefficients. The reference group (omitted group) has these attributes: male, four years of college, nonveteran, year 2002, and states in the lowest of the seven top-code threshold categories we define. The data are at the individual level by year, though "i" and "t" subscripts are omitted from the specification above. The Tobit regression provides coefficient estimates as well as an estimate of the standard deviation of the error term.

We used the Tobit results to predict earnings by percentile. Consider earnings at the 70th percentile, meaning that 70 percent of the population of interest (e.g., psychologists) have earnings less than the earnings at this percentile. Then, if $X'\beta$ is the earnings index from the Tobit regression and σ is the standard deviation of the error term, it follows that

$$0.7 = \Phi\left(\frac{z_{0.7} - X'\beta}{\sigma}\right),$$

where $z_{0.7}$ is the earnings level at the 70th percentile and Φ is the normal distribution. We obtain predicted earnings at the 70th percentile as $z_{0.7} = \sigma\Phi^{-1}(0.7) + X'\beta$. As an alternative, we explored using quantile regression to estimate the earnings percentiles. We did not find an estimation routine that controlled for censoring, however, and estimates showed a lack of smoothness in the upper quantiles, perhaps because of the lack of control for censoring.

Results

The Tobit estimates are tabled in Appendix E, along with variable means and standard deviations. The following points summarize findings that were consistent across the estimates:

- Earnings increase quadratically with age and typically peak at ages in the mid-50s.
- In most occupations, earnings of workers with more than four years of college are 15 to 25 percent higher than earnings of workers with four years of college. The exception is occupational therapists, for whom there is no earnings premium. This comparison is beside the point for physicians, 99 percent of whom report more than four years of college.
- Compared with males, females earn 4 percent less as social workers; 10 to 17 percent less as psychologists, registered nurses, occupational therapists, and physician assistants; and nearly 30 percent less as physicians and in non–mental health professions in general.
- Veteran earnings are generally within a few percentage points of nonveteran earnings. There are some differences across the occupations, but the veteran parameter estimates are often not statistically significant.
- Compared with the reference year, 2002, earnings in other years are higher for physicians, psychologists, registered nurses, occupational therapists, and physician assistants but

lower for social workers and non–mental health professionals. Broadly speaking, health profession earnings recovered from the recession in 2002 and did not decrease in the Great Recession beginning in 2008, whereas non–health profession earnings remained several percentage points below their 2002 level.

- Top-code controls are statistically significant, indicating their role in controlling against possible downward bias in earnings profiles.
- The standard deviation of the error in the earnings regression is greatest for physicians. This is not surprising, given the wide range of earnings across physician specialties compared with other occupations.

Predicted earnings by age for the 40th through 90th earnings percentiles are shown in Figures 5.1 through 5.7. The values of the explanatory variables used in making the predictions are male, more than four years of college, year 2011, and veteran who left the military in 2001 to 2012, and the predictions are in 2013 dollars. Predicted earnings are displayed for ages 30 to 65. Physician earnings are highest among our occupations, followed by occupations with fairly similar earnings, physician assistants, psychologists, and registered nurses. The remaining two occupations, occupational therapists and social workers, have somewhat lower earnings. Figure 5.7 shows predicted earnings for full-time, full-year workers with four or more years of college who are not in our mental health care occupations. Their mean earnings reach a maximum of $100,000 at ages 50 to 55.

Physicians' maximum mean earnings are $374,000 at age 54. Interestingly, median earnings at that age are $217,000. Mean earnings are higher than median earnings because earnings are distributed log normally; unlogged earnings have a fat right tail. Only for physicians

Figure 5.1
Predicted Earnings, by Age: Physicians (2013 $)

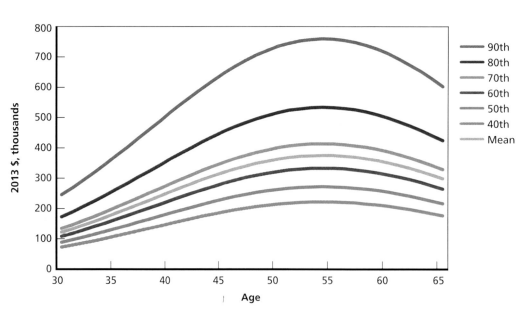

SOURCE: Earnings regressions of ACS data for full-time, full-year, college-educated workers from 2003 through 2012.
RAND RR1425-5.1

Figure 5.2
Predicted Earnings, by Age: Psychologists (2013 $)

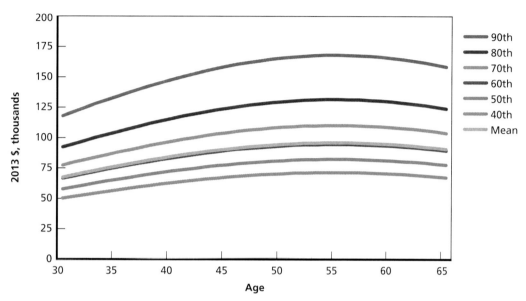

SOURCE: Earnings regressions of ACS data for full-time, full-year, college-educated workers from 2003 through 2012.
RAND *RR1425-5.2*

Figure 5.3
Predicted Earnings, by Age: Registered Nurses (2013 $)

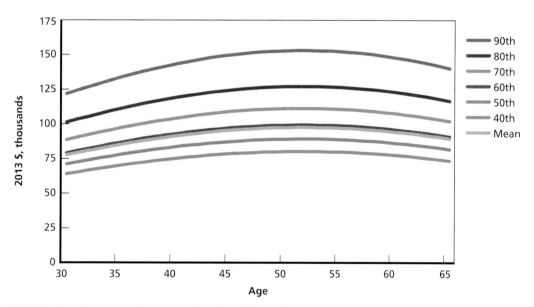

SOURCE: Earnings regressions of ACS data for full-time, full-year, college-educated workers from 2003 through 2012.
RAND *RR1425-5.3*

Figure 5.4
Predicted Earnings, by Age: Physician Assistants (2013 $)

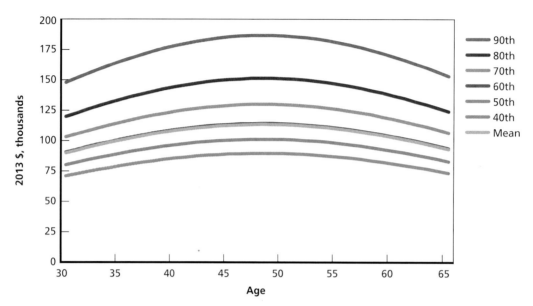

SOURCE: Earnings regressions of ACS data for full-time, full-year, college-educated workers from 2003 through 2012.
RAND RR1425-5.4

Figure 5.5
Predicted Earnings, by Age: Occupational Therapists (2013 $)

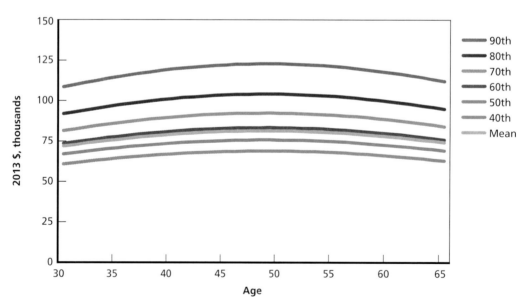

SOURCE: Earnings regressions of ACS data for full-time, full-year, college-educated workers from 2003 through 2012.
RAND RR1425-5.5

Figure 5.6
Predicted Earnings, by Age: Social Workers (2013 $)

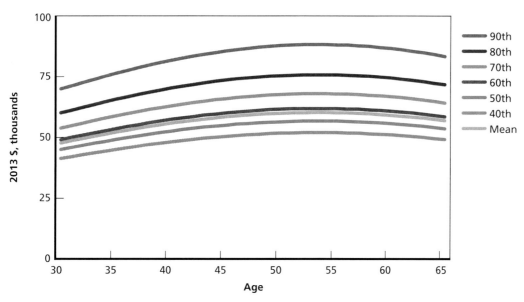

SOURCE: Earnings regressions of ACS data for full-time, full-year, college-educated workers from 2003 through 2012.
RAND *RR1425-5.6*

Figure 5.7
Predicted Earnings, by Age: Non–Mental Health Care Workers (2013 $)

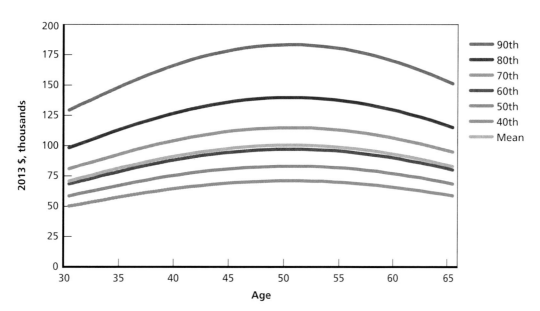

SOURCE: Earnings regressions of ACS data for full-time, full-year, college-educated workers from 2003 through 2012.
RAND *RR1425-5.7*

are mean earnings above the 60th percentile and are roughly at the 65th percentile. Mean earnings in the other occupations are close to the 60th percentile.

Predicted earnings decline after ages in the mid-50s. This may reflect fewer hours of work among these full-time workers. For example, based on our tabulations the usual weekly hours of work for full-time, full-year physicians averaged 58.4 hours for ages 30–39, 57.0 hours for ages 40–49, and 54.8 hours for ages 50–59. Other factors could be involved, too. One conjecture is that lifecycle earnings are higher for more recent-entry cohorts. But the physician earnings distribution has been fairly stable since the mid-1990s, at least in the lower half. Seabury, Jena, and Chandra (2013) found no significant growth in median annual earnings for physicians from 1996–2000 to 2006–2010. Seabury, Jena, and Chandra used Current Population Survey (CPS; U.S. Census Bureau, no date-b) data but did not limit the sample to full-time, full-year physicians. In separate CPS tabulations (not shown) limited to full-time, full-year physicians, we found no growth or decline in physician earnings over these years for earnings in the 10th through 50th deciles. Tabulated earnings at higher deciles are problematic because of top-coding.

Psychiatrist Earnings

ACS data do not identify physicians by specialty. To address this limitation, we used OES and AMGA data to learn approximately where psychiatrist earnings lie in the physician earnings distribution. We describe our approach to handling OES and AMGA data and present a table with earnings by specialty for specialties covered by both OES and AMGA.

OES data provide average hourly wage and average annual earnings for a variety of specialties, including psychiatrists. OES collects employment data from a sample of establishments. The data contain the number of workers in a given wage interval in a narrowly defined occupation. The average wage in each wage interval is calculated from the NCS. The overall average wage is the total weighted hourly wages for an occupation divided by its weighted survey employment (Bureau of Labor Statistics, no date-a).[4] To estimate annual earnings, OES multiplies the average hourly wage by 2,080 hours (52 weeks × 40 hours) per year (Bureau of Labor Statistics, no date-a). That is, annual earnings are for a full-year, full-time employee; OES annual earnings can be described as annualized hourly wages. Employees might work more or fewer than 2,080 hours, but OES annual earnings do not capture this fact. Also, OES data include residents on hospital staffs. Residents earn less than fully trained physicians, and including them decreases average annual earnings.

We adjust OES earnings with average weekly hours to obtain a more accurate view of annual earnings. We tabulated hours from March CPS data and found that full-time, full-year, trained physicians worked 56.2 hours per week in 2001 and 53.4 hours per week in 2010.[5] The

---

[4] Further methodological details may be relevant. The surveyed establishment reports the annual salary for workers who are paid an annual salary but do not work full-time, full-year. The hourly wage cannot be computed for these workers because the OES does not collect data on hours. Some physicians might be salaried and work part-year or part-time for a health care organization and would fall into this category. We avoid this ambiguity in our analysis of CPS data, which we limit to full-time, full-year workers.

[5] To obtain a sample of trained physicians, we trimmed the sample by eliminating physicians at ages 17–35 with incomes of $60,000 or less. The eliminated physicians were likely to be in training at an internship, residency, or fellowship (post-residency training in a subspecialty).

latter is a third higher than a 40-hour week, the former even more. As a result, our adjusted OES estimates of physician annual earnings are that much higher than the published OES figures.

We use data from the 2010 AMGA survey of its medical group members for estimates of median physician income by specialty. In the AMGA survey, 239 groups responded and 57 percent of these groups had more than 100 providers, the largest group size category. More than 91 percent of providers were in these groups; that is, 47,240 of 51,758 total providers were in groups with more than 100 providers. This implies that the median physician compensation reported by AMGA lies among these large groups.[6]

Table 5.1 combines AMGA data on median compensation and our adjusted OES data on average earnings for the specialties covered by OES. The estimates are fairly close.[7] OES and AMGA data indicate that psychiatrists are paid similarly to family practitioners, internists, and pediatricians and have annual earnings of about $225,000, i.e., a value between the AMGA estimate of $217,000 and the OES estimate of $232,000.

Figure 5.8 shows median compensation by specialty from the AMGA survey. Psychiatry is in the lower portion of the earnings spectrum. Its near neighbors are family medicine,

Table 5.1
Annual Physician Earnings for Comparable AMGA and OES Specialties, 2010

Specialty	AMGA	OES
Pediatricians, general	$213,379	$225,106
Psychiatrists	$217,169	$232,473
Family and general practitioners	$208,658	$236,691
Internists, general	$219,500	$252,548
Obstetricians and gynecologists	$302,638	$291,790
Surgeons[a]	$359,106	$309,061
Anesthesiologists	$372,750	$313,600

SOURCE: Estimated annual physician earnings based on AMGA and OES data.

NOTES: For OES, reported figures reflect the product of mean hourly wage, CPS average physician hours in 2010 (53.39 hours), and 52 weeks. For AMGA, reported figures reflect median compensation.

[a] For surgeons, the AMGA figure reflects a weighted average of surgical specialties in AMGA data using AMGA counts by specialty.

---

[6] The respondents (groups) report the annual compensation

for each physician from each specialty on the specialty code list. Compensation is the annual salary of the physician based on the current compensation rate plus any deferred compensation, tax-deferred annuities, and/or anticipated cash distributions during the upcoming 12 months based on prior year performance, but excluding any payments under normal retirement, pension, or profit-sharing plans. Full-time equivalent (FTE) physicians with at least a 0.5 clinical FTE are reported at their actual compensation amount. (AMGA, 2011)

[7] The AMGA data are for median compensation, and the OES are mean earnings. From the log-linearity of the earnings distribution, we expect median earnings to be less than mean earnings, other things equal. Hence, we might expect the AMGA value to be less than the OES value for a given specialty. Table 4.1 shows that AMGA compensation is in fact less than OES earnings for pediatricians, psychiatrists, family and general practitioners, and internists. But AMGA compensation is higher than OES earnings for surgeons and anesthesiologists, contrary to expectation. We do not know the reasons for this. Perhaps medical groups pay a premium to the surgeons and anesthesiologists they employ, or perhaps the AMGA sample of these specialties is small or unrepresentative.

Figure 5.8
AMGA Physician Median Compensation by Specialty, 2010 (2011 $, thousands)

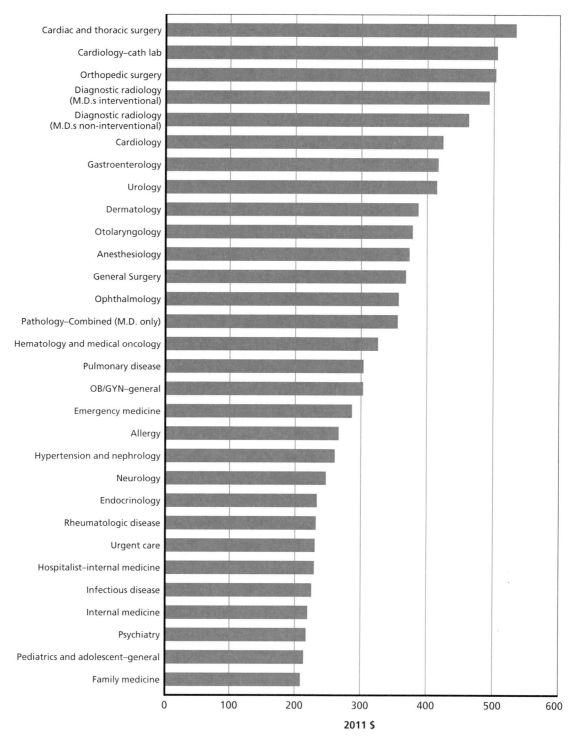

SOURCE: Estimated median compensation for civilian physicians by medical specialty, based on AMGA survey data.
RAND *RR1425-5.8*

pediatrics and adolescent–general, internal medicine, infectious disease, and urgent care, and compensation for these specialties ranges from $209,000 to $230,000. Other specialties pay more, from rheumatologic disease at $232,000 up to orthopedic surgery, cardiology–cath lab, and cardiac and thoracic surgery, with median compensation around $500,000.

To compare the value of $225,000 with the earnings deciles for physicians in Figure 5.1, we first need to adjust for the fact that the $225,000 is an overall average for male and female physicians, whereas the earnings deciles are for male physicians. The overall average of $225,000 corresponds to male physician earnings of $247,000.[8] We take the average age of physicians to be 45 (Table E.1). At this age, $247,000 lies between the 50th and 60th deciles and (from computation not shown) is between the 53rd and 54th percentiles. Based on this, we conclude that we can use predicted earnings of physicians at the 50th or 60th decile to approximate the expected civilian earnings of male military psychiatrists.

With respect to female military psychiatrists, we assume that they have the same expected civilian earnings opportunities as male military psychiatrists. The assumption in effect has two parts: female and male physicians face the same civilian pay scale and employers provide the same opportunity to choose hours of work. Several peer-reviewed studies are relevant to the assumption (Appendix F). Lo Sasso et al. (2011) finds a relatively small difference in starting salaries between male and female physicians. Weeks, Wallace, and Wallace (2009) controls for specialty, board certification, and years of practice but not hours of work finds lower earnings for female physicians, similar to our regression results. Baker's (1996) study of physicians with two to nine years of practice controls for practice setting, specialty, and hours of work finds no difference in earnings. The studies suggest that male/female differences in hours of work are critical to understanding the difference in male/female earnings. The assumption that employers provide the same opportunity to choose hours of work is an employer-side assumption. It is meant to differentiate from factors that might affect female versus male physicians' supply of hours. For instance, family responsibilities might be greater and more constraining for females.

Summary

We estimated Tobit regressions for each of our health professions with ACS data for 2002 to 2012 and used them to predict earnings by age, by percentile of earnings (Figures 5.1–5.7). The predicted earnings are inputs to the DRM.

Because ACS data do not identify physicians by specialty, we relied on auxiliary data to determine that earnings for male psychiatrists lie between the 50th and 60th percentiles of the earnings distribution for male physicians. Also, the regressions indicated lower earnings for female than male physicians, which led to the question of which civilian earnings percentile to use for female military psychiatrists. Peer-reviewed studies found that differences in male/female earnings depend on differences in practice setting, specialty, and hours of work. Under the assumption that female and male military physicians share the same choice set of practice

---

[8] We know that $\bar{w} = \theta w^m + (1-\theta)w^f$, where θ is the fraction of physicians that are male. We know from the regression results that female physicians earn less than male physicians, other things equal: $w^f = \alpha w^m$, where $0 < \alpha < 1$. From the table of means (Table E.1), $\theta=0.7$, and from the regression for physicians (Table E.2), female physicians earn 30 percent less than male physicians, so $\alpha=0.7$. Using these values, an average wage of $225,000 corresponds to a male wage of $247,000.

settings, job openings by specialty, and hours of work, we use the male earnings percentile for both male and female military psychiatrists.

CHAPTER SIX

Dynamic Retention Model Parameter Estimation

In this chapter, we describe our estimation methodology, longitudinal data on retention, DRM parameter estimates, and model fit for the mental health professions we study.

Estimation Methodology

To estimate DRMs for the mental health professions, we use the mathematical structure of the model together with assumptions on the distributions of tastes across members and shocks. This allows us to derive expressions for the transition probabilities, given one's state, which are then used to compose an expression for the likelihood of each individual's years of active retention and reserve participation. Importantly, each transition probability is itself a function of the underlying parameters of the DRM. These are the parameters of the taste distribution, the shock distributions, the switching costs, and the discount factor. The estimation routine finds parameter values that maximize the likelihood.

The transition probability is the probability in a given period of choosing a particular alternative, i.e., active, reserve, or civilian, given one's state. Because we assume that the model is first-order Markov,[1] that the shocks have extreme value distributions, and that the shocks are uncorrelated from year to year, we can derive closed form expressions for each transition probability. For example, as Train (2009) shows, the probability of choosing to stay active at time t, given the member is already in the active component, is given by the logistic form

$$Pr(V^A > V^L) = \frac{e^{\frac{V^A}{\kappa}}}{e^{\frac{V^A}{\kappa}} + \left[e^{\frac{V^R}{\lambda}} + e^{\frac{V^C}{\lambda}} \right]^{\frac{\lambda}{\kappa}}}.$$

We omit the subscripts for individual i and year t for clarity. We can also obtain expressions for the probability of leaving the active component and, having left, the probabilities of entering, or staying in, the reserve component in each subsequent year. To relate the DRM to discrete choice models, we note that in a given period and for a given state and individual taste, the individual's value functions for staying and leaving have the same form as those of a random

---

[1] This means that all relevant information from past outcomes is represented in the current state vector, which in our case includes years of active component service, years of reserve service, and taste.

utility model. Similarly, for those who have left active duty, the choices of whether to enter the reserves or to remain in the reserves are also based on a random utility model. More broadly, the reserve choice is nested in the choice to leave active duty, and the model has a nested logit form. (See Train [2009] for further discussion.) Of course, the DRM differs from a traditional random utility model because the explanatory variables are value functions, not simple variables such as age and education, and the value functions are recursive.

The transition probabilities in different periods are independent and can be multiplied together to obtain the probability of any given individual's career profile of active, reserve, and civilian states that we observe in the data. Multiplying the career profile probabilities together gives an expression for the sample likelihood that we use to estimate the model parameters for each occupation using maximum likelihood methods. Optimization is done using the Broyden-Fletcher-Goldfarb-Shanno (BFGS) algorithm, a standard hill-climbing method. We compute standard errors of the estimates using numerical differentiation of the likelihood function and taking the square root of the absolute value of the diagonal of the inverse of the Hessian matrix. To judge goodness of fit, we use parameter estimates to simulate retention profiles for synthetic individuals (characterized by tastes drawn from the taste distribution) who are subject to shocks (drawn from the shock distributions), then aggregate the individual profiles to obtain a force-level retention curve and compare it with the retention curve computed from actual data.

As discussed in Chapter Three, the estimation code for psychiatrists considers the choice of a two-, three-, or four-year MSP obligation. The logistic functional form of the model, shown above, follows from an assumption about the error terms of the stay and leave value functions. The errors are assumed to be distributed extreme-value with zero shape parameter and the same scale parameter. In the model without the MSP nest, the scale of the error in the value function for leaving is $\kappa = \sqrt{\lambda^2 + \tau^2}$, which we now relabel as $\kappa = \sqrt{\lambda_1^2 + \tau_1^2}$. By similar logic, the scale in the value function for staying with the MSP nest may be written $\sqrt{\lambda_2^2 + \tau_2^2}$. Imposing the requirement that the scales be equal, which is necessary to obtain the logit form for the probability, we also set $\kappa = \sqrt{\lambda_2^2 + \tau_2^2}$. When estimating the model, we estimate κ, λ_1, and λ_2 and infer τ_1 and τ_2, respectively, from $\kappa = \sqrt{\lambda_1^2 + \tau_1^2}$ and $\kappa = \sqrt{\lambda_2^2 + \tau_2^2}$.

Most paths from the MSP choice have a near-zero probability. We exploit this fact in our calculations by noting that if one term of a product of probabilities is zero, the entire expression is zero. This saves us from having to explicitly calculate the other terms in the cumulative probability expression.

We estimate the following model parameters:

- the mean and standard deviation of tastes for active and reserve service relative to civilian opportunities (e.g., μ_a, μ_r, σ_a, and σ_r). The correlation between active and reserve taste is assume to be 1.
- a scale parameter for the shocks to the value functions for staying and for the reserve/civilian nest, κ.
- a scale parameter for the shock affecting the reserve and civilian states individually (λ_1)
- for psychiatrists only, a scale parameter for the shock affecting the MSP contract length choices (λ_2)
- a switching cost incurred if the individual leaves active duty before completing ADSO
- a switching cost incurred if the individual leaves active and reserve duty before serving a combined total service obligation

- a switching cost incurred if the individual moves from "civilian" to "reserve"[2]
- a personal discount factor.[3]

Once we have parameter estimates for a well-fitting model, we can use the logic of the model and the estimated parameters to simulate the active component cumulative probability of retention to each YOS in the steady state for a given policy environment, such as the introduction of a new S&I pay or a change in the level of the pay. By steady state, we mean when all members have spent their entire careers are under the policy environment being considered. The simulation output includes a graph of the active component retention profile by YOS. We can also produce graphs of reserve component participation and provide computations of costs, though we do not do so here. We show model fit by simulating the steady-state retention profile in the current policy environment and comparing it with the retention profile observed in the data.

Our use of the term "steady state" differs from usage in dynamic models where it refers to point(s) such that the vector of state variables, regardless of starting value, has converged to a value that is unchanging over time. The system is said to be in a steady state when the state vector regenerates itself period after period. In our use, the retention profile is in a steady state when it would be realized for successive entering cohorts. This occurs when every cohort has the same taste distribution, shock distributions, and same personnel management and compensation policy. In other research (Asch, Mattock, and Hosek, 2013), we study the effect of introducing a new policy and allowing incumbent personnel to opt in to the new policy or remain under the baseline policy. The overall retention curve evolves from the curve under the baseline policy to the curve under the new policy as more and more cohorts enter under the new policy and depending on how many incumbent personnel opt in. Finally, a maintained assumption in our analyses is that the taste and shock distributions and personnel management policy remain the same from cohort to cohort. As a result, the retention profile (the percentage retained to each YOS) would be the same from cohort to cohort so long as the compensation policy remained the same. Notably, the retention profile would not depend on the size of the cohort. We recognize that policy changes could change the taste distribution of entering cohorts and perhaps change the shock distribution. For instance, a large increase in the size of an entering cohort might decrease the cohort's mean taste for military service.

Longitudinal Data on Retention

DMDC's Work Experience File data contain person-specific longitudinal records of active and reserve service. Work Experience File data begin with service members in the active or reserve component on or after September 30, 1990. Our analysis file for each occupation includes active component officer entrants in 1990–2000, as discussed above. The entrants are followed

---

[2] In initial work for psychiatrists, this second switch cost was consistently not statistically significant. We therefore constrained this switch cost to be zero for this group. However, we estimate this parameter for the other mental health provider models.

[3] The exceptions are the psychiatrist model and the psychologist model. We fixed the personal discount rates in these models because we found the model fits were better and parameter estimates were more reasonable relative to our expectations based on past research. We set the personal discount factor in this model equal to 0.94, which is the value we have typically estimated for officers in earlier work. For other health professionals, the discount factor is estimated.

through 2010, providing 21 years of data for the 1990 cohort and ten years of data for the 2000 cohort. We estimated the DRM for the 1990–2000 entering cohorts of psychiatrists and psychologists "entering" at the O-3 level, and of occupational therapists, physician assistants, and social workers entering at the O-1 level. For nurses, we estimate models with data on all nurses from the 1990–2000 cohorts and on the subset of nurses ever identified as mental health nurses. The model structure differed in some cases across the occupations to account for their specific career paths, so the data construction differed in some cases as well.

Parameter Estimates for Psychiatrists

We estimated DRMs for the two largest groups of psychiatrists, HPSPs and USUHS grads. The HSPC model is for psychiatrists who received an HPSP scholarship along with a four-year military residency who incur either a three- or four-year total ADSO. The restriction on service obligation automatically limits the sample to psychiatrists without existing undergraduate obligations for military service as would come from ROTC scholarships or attending a service academy. We also limit the sample to psychiatrists who did not have prior active or reserve duty experience, in order to focus on cohorts that first entered military service through their medical education.

This first group was estimated using a sample of 158 psychiatrists from the 1990–2000 entry cohorts. Among the 158 psychiatrists, 63 received four years of HPSP support. These psychiatrists incurred four years of obligation for their HPSP support and three years of obligation for their residencies. Because these obligations could be concurrently paid off, they were first able to make a voluntary retention decision after eight years of service. The remaining 95 psychiatrists incurred two to three years of obligation for their HPSP support, and three years of obligation for their residencies. Thus, they had a three-year active duty obligation and could first make a voluntary retention decision after seven years of service, again assuming a military residency.

Second, we estimated the model for psychiatrists who attended USUHS, completed a four-year military residency, and had a seven-year obligation. As with HPSP recipients, we limited the sample to psychiatrists who did not have prior active or reserve duty experience. This model was estimated on a sample of 33 psychiatrists from the 1990–2000 cohorts. These psychiatrists could first make a voluntary retention decision 11 years after starting their residencies.

The military pay line we use in the estimation for psychiatrists includes RMC, VSP, ASP, and BCP, as well as the expected value of ISP. We model the MSP choice, so this is not included in the pay line.

Table 6.1 shows the parameter estimates and standard errors. In the HPSP model, we find that all of the parameters are statistically different from zero, with the exception of the standard deviation of reserve taste. In the USUHS model, a number of the parameters are not significant. The lack of statistical significance is not surprising, given the small sample size and the individual selectivity in choosing USHUS with its long obligation. The estimates are denominated in thousands of 2009 dollars, except for the assumed discount rate.[4]

We find that mean active taste is negative. For HPSP recipients, mean active taste is equal to about –$140,000. A negative value for mean taste is consistent with past studies estimating the mean active taste among military officers and suggests that the military must offer relatively

---

[4] The personal discount factor is the inverse of 1 plus the personal discount rate: $1/(1 + d)$.

Table 6.1
Parameter Estimates and Standard Errors: HPSP Psychiatrists with Four-Year Military Residency and Three- or Four-Year ADSO and USUHS Psychiatrists with Four-Year Military Residency and Seven-Year ADSO

Coefficient	HPSP		USUHS	
	Estimate	Standard Error	Estimate	Standard Error
Shape Parameter, Total Error = τ	141.9	70.4	176.9	96.0
Shape Parameter, Alternatives Within Nest = λ_1	14.6	2.1	10.6	6.2
Shape Parameter, MSP Alternatives = λ_2	14.7	5.1	8.4	7.5
Mean Active Taste = μ_a	−139.7	43.5	−57.8	46.1
Mean Reserve Taste = μ_r	−24.6	0.8	−29.6	6.8
SD Active Taste = σ_a	77.3	46.0	103.2	120.4
SD Reserve Taste = σ_r	1.3	1.4	1.1	8.0
Switch Cost: Leave Active < ADSO	−233.2	111.2	−185.0	162.5
Switch Cost: Switch from Civilian to Reserve	−91.8	11.8	−146.8	72.3
Personal Discount Factor (Assumed)	0.94	N/A	0.94	N/A
−1*Log Likelihood	627.8		72.6	
N	158		33	

SOURCE: Parameter estimates from cohorts of psychiatrists entering active duty between 1990 and 2000.

NOTES: Sample is restricted to individuals whose career histories indicated that they performed a four-year military residency and had either (1) a three- or four-year ADSO, in the case of HPSP graduates, or (2) a seven-year ADSO, in the case of USUHS graduates. The shape parameter κ governs the shocks to the value functions for staying and for the reserve/civilian nest, while λ_1 governs the shocks affecting the civilian and reserve nests individually, and λ_2 governs the shock affecting the MSP nest. The means and standard deviations of tastes for active and reserve service relative to civilian opportunities are estimated, as are the costs associated with leaving active duty before completing ADSO, and for switching from civilian status to participating in the reserves. The second switch cost parameter was set to zero and the personal discount factor was assumed to be 0.94 in these models.

high pay to compensate for the requirements of service on active duty relative to not being in the military. We expected the longer ADSO for attending USUHS to attract individuals with higher taste for military service. Consistent with this, the mean active taste among USUHS graduates is substantially greater, −$58,000, and is not statistically different from zero.

The standard deviation of active duty taste is $77,300 for HPSP recipients and $103,200 for USUHS graduates. The model structure assumes tastes are normally distributed, which implies that 68 percent of the tastes are within plus-or-minus one standard deviation of the mean taste, and 95 percent are within two standard deviations. Thus, the estimated standard deviation of the taste distribution for psychiatrists is such that 68 percent lie in the range of −$140,000 ± $77,300 for HPSP recipients and −$58,000 ± $103,200 for USUHS graduates. In other words, many USUHS graduates have a positive taste for military service.

Mean taste for reserve duty is also negative and is similar for both groups: −$24,600 for HPSP recipients and −$29,600 for USUHS graduates. Interestingly, mean taste for reserve duty is less negative than mean taste for active duty for HPSP recipients, but is approximately the same as mean taste for active duty for USUHS graduates. The estimate for the standard deviation of reserve taste is quite low (1.3 for HPSP and 1.1 for USUHS). By comparison, the "within nest" scale parameter for the reserve/civilian nest is much larger (14.6 for HPSP and 10.6 for USUHS). This scale parameter reflects the standard deviation of the shock terms for the "reserve" and "civilian" alternatives. In particular, given that the shocks are distributed Extreme Value Type I, the standard deviation equals the scale parameter times $\pi / \sqrt{6} \approx 1.28$. The results suggest that movement into and out of the reserve and civilian statuses is largely driven by random shocks rather than by diverse tastes among members.

The other "within nest" scale parameter is for the MSP nest. This parameter is relative large, 14.7, and highly statistically significant for HPSP. This implies that the standard deviation of the shock to the MSP nest is 18.8 ($= 1.28 \times 14.7$) for HPSP and 10.8 ($= 1.28 \times 8.4$) for USUHS. The scale parameter of the total shock, κ, is \$141,900 and is statistically significant at the 5 percent level for HPSP. It is \$176,900 and significant at the 10 percent level for USUHS. The relatively large size of the κ compared with either of the scale parameters associated with the within-nest shock terms, λ_1 or λ_2, implies that the scale parameters associated with the common shock across the reserve and civilian nest, τ_1, and across the MSP contract-length nest, τ_2, account for relatively large shares of the total shock.

The switching costs for leaving active duty early are approximately –\$233,200 for HPSP and –\$285,000 for USUHS. The cost of switching back to a reserve component after being a civilian is not as large but still sizable (–\$91,800 for HPSP and –\$146,800 for USUHS). The high cost of leaving active duty early may reflect the fact that those who leave early may be required to repay scholarship money or other financial or in-kind assistance. The high cost of switching to the reserve component after being civilian may reflect the difficulty of finding an available reserve position or implicit costs to one's civilian career. Few individuals make this switch in the data.

Chapter Four discussed psychiatrist S&I pay for 2000 and 2009 and presented a figure showing inflation-adjusted S&I from 1993 to 2015. In particular, MSP increased by up to \$8,000 per year for a two-year contract, \$18,000 per year for a three-year contract, and \$29,000 per year for a four-year contract. We used the higher 2009 values for MSP in estimating the DRM. To check the robustness of results, we also estimated the model using the 2000 MSP values. Though those results are not shown, we found that the model fit for psychiatrists was as good in Figure 6.1 as under this alternative assumption.

Model Fit for Psychiatrists

Figure 6.1 shows the model fit for HPSP psychiatrists, and Figure 6.2 shows it for USUHS psychiatrists. The red line is the simulated retention profile, and the black line is the retention profile observed in the data. The dotted lines show the confidence interval for the observed data. In Chapter Seven, we simulate retention for alternative compensation scenarios through YOS 30, but since our data extend at most 20 years, here we simulate retention only through YOS 20.

In both the active and reserve graphs, the horizontal axis counts years since the individual was observed beginning a military residency. In the active graph, the vertical axis shows the cumulative probability of retention on active duty until that year. In the reserve graph, the vertical axis shows the cumulative probability of being in reserve service but not active service

Figure 6.1
Model Fit Results: HPSP Psychiatrists with Four-Year Military Residency and Three- to Four-Year Service Obligation

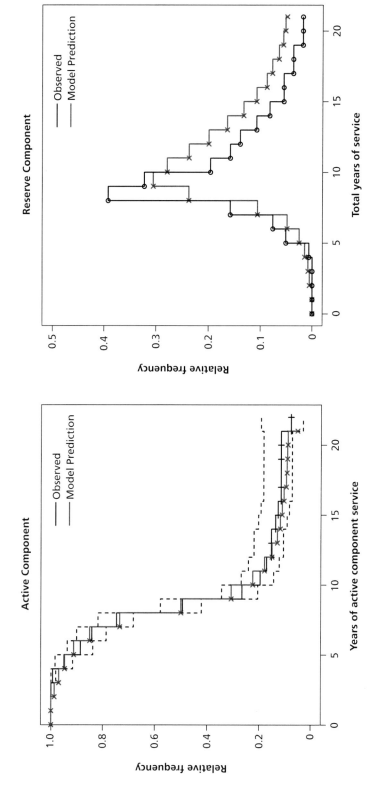

NOTES: The left panel shows the observed Kaplan-Meier survival curve and simulated active duty survival curve based on estimates for psychiatrists who entered through the HPSP program, and who had three to four years' ADSO and three to four years' military residency. The panel on the right shows the observed histogram and simulated reserve participation histogram for these psychiatrists.

Figure 6.2
Model Fit Results: USUHS Psychiatrists with Four-Year Military Residency and Seven-Year Service Obligation

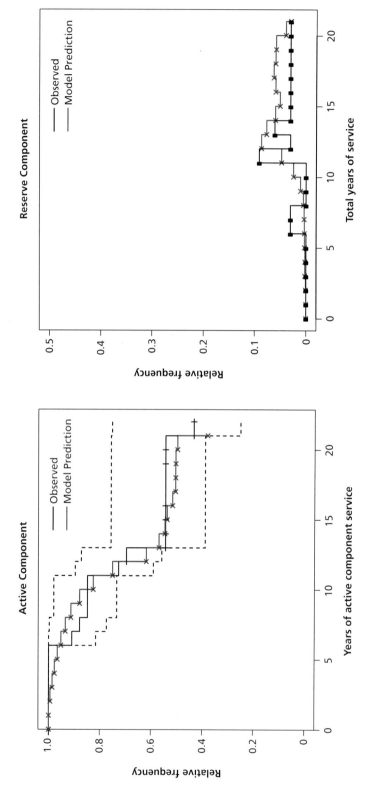

NOTES: The left panel shows the observed Kaplan-Meier survival curve and simulated active duty survival curve based on estimates for psychiatrists who attended USUHS, and who had seven years' ADSO and four years' military residency. The panel on the right shows the observed histogram and simulated reserve participation histogram for these psychiatrists.

RAND *RR1425-6.2*

in that year (that is, the cumulative probability of being in the active or reserve service, minus the probability of being in the active service). The solid black line shows the actual retention of individuals in our cohorts, and the red line shows the predicted retention.

The model fit for the active component is quite good for both samples and well within the error bands. Consistent with longer ADSO and higher taste for military service, USUHS graduates are much more likely to stay on active duty than HPSP candidates for any given year of service. As expected, we observe sharp drop-offs in retention in the first year in which psychiatrists are eligible to make voluntary retention decisions (seven to eight years for HPSP psychiatrists, 11 years for USUHS graduates).

The model fit for the reserve component is not as good. This reflects the small sample size of psychiatrists and the fact that relatively few affiliate with the reserves. The simulations focus on the active component where the fit is much better.

Parameter Estimates for Other Mental Health Care Providers

HPSP is available to psychologists and nurses, and USUHS offers programs for psychologists. The services also offer a variety of training programs for nurses, occupational therapists, and physician assistants. However, our analysis of the career patterns exhibited by the 1990–2000 cohorts suggested that most are direct accessions. Out of 515 psychologists, only 42 appear to have been in the HPSP program based on time spent at grade O-1 on reserve duty, and none were flagged as having attended USUHS. Among 8,228 nurses, 50 were flagged as attending USUHS, and fewer than 400 were flagged as potentially being part of HPSP. While some may have attended other training programs, we are unable to identify this in the data. We thus assumed that all individuals were direct accessions with a three-year ADSO.

The sample sizes for cohorts from 1990–2000 included 515 psychologists; 8,228 nurses, of whom 212 were flagged as mental health nurses at least once; 137 occupational therapists; 132 physician assistants; and 287 social workers. We further limited the samples to individuals with no prior active or reserve duty, who were identified as being direct accessions, and who had three years of ADSO. Given the small numbers of occupational therapists and physician assistants, as well as their identical military pay lines and similar length of training requirements (one to two years post-baccalaureate), we estimated a single model for the two occupations.

Table 6.2 presents empirical results for each occupation. To make the numerical optimization easier, we did not estimate the parameters directly, but instead estimated the logarithm of each parameter. To recover the parameter estimates, we transformed the estimates. Table 6.3 shows the transformed parameter estimates for each occupation. Nearly all of the parameters are statistically significant, many highly significant.

Mean taste for active duty service varies across occupations.[5] The mean tastes are −$73,700 for psychologists, −$30,000 for mental health nurses, −$10,000 for all nurses, and −$22,200 for social workers. The parameter estimate for mean active duty taste is small and statistically indistinguishable from zero for occupational therapists and physician assistants. The standard deviation of active duty taste ranges from $11,000 for social workers to $54,600 for psycholo-

---

[5] The version of the model here constrained mean taste to be negative. However, we experimented with various specifications that allowed mean taste to be positive or negative, and did not find positive taste.

Table 6.2
Parameter Estimates and Standard Errors for Other Mental Health Care Provider Occupations

Coefficient	Psychologists		Mental Health Nurses		All Nurses		Occupational Therapists, Physician Assistants		Social Workers	
	Estimate	Standard Error	Estimate	Standard Error	Estimate	Standard Error	Estimate	Standard Error	Estimate	Standard Error
ln(Shape Parameter, nest error) =ln(τ)	1.3	25.4	-1.1	203.1	-1.0	17.4	-1.1	364.4	-1.1	186.1
ln(Shape Parameter, Alternatives within Nest) = ln(λ)	5.1	0.2	4.6	0.5	4.4	0.1	5.2	0.6	5.2	0.4
ln(−1*Mean Active Taste) = ln(μ_a)	4.3	0.1	3.4	0.8	2.3	0.3	-3.0	38.5	3.1	1.1
ln(−1*Mean Reserve Taste) = ln(μ_r)	3.9	0.1	3.1	0.6	2.6	0.1	3.0	0.6	3.4	0.6
ln(SD Active Taste) = ln(σ_a)	4.0	0.4	3.0	0.8	3.1	0.1	3.5	1.0	2.4	2.4
ln(SD Reserve Taste) = ln(σ_r)	1.7	38.9	1.4	3.4	1.0	8.6	-0.7	31.5	2.8	0.9
ln(−1*Leave Active <3 Years)	6.4	0.2	5.6	0.5	5.4	0.1	4.8	0.7	4.4	0.6
ln(−1*Leave Reserve)	6.1	0.2	4.7	0.6	4.9	0.1	5.7	0.6	5.9	0.4
ln(−1*Switch from Civilian to Reserve)	6.9	0.2	6.6	0.5	6.4	0.1	7.2	0.6	7.2	0.4
Personal Discount Factor	0.94 (assumed)	N/A	2.4	0.6	2.0	0.1	2.1	0.3	2.2	0.4
−1*Log Likelihood	1,920		720		28,196		873		1,114	
N	453		157		6.154		184		246	

SOURCE: Parameter estimates from cohorts of mental health providers entering active duty between 1990 and 2000.

NOTES: The shape parameter κ governs the shocks to the value functions for staying and for the reserve/civilian nest, while λ governs the shocks affecting the civilian and reserve nests individually. The means and standard deviations of tastes for active and reserve service relative to civilian opportunities are estimated, as are the costs associated with leaving active duty before serving at least three years, for leaving the reserves, and for switching from civilian status to participating in the reserves. The personal discount factor was assumed to be 0.94 for psychologists.

Table 6.3
Transformed Parameter Estimates for Other Mental Health Care Provider Occupations

Parameter	Psychologists	Mental Health Nurses	All Nurses	Occupational Therapists, Physician Assistants	Social Workers
Shape Parameter, nest error = τ	3.7	0.3	0.4	0.3	0.3
Shape Parameter, Alternatives within Nest = λ_1	164.0	99.5	81.5	181.3	181.3
Mean Active Taste = μ_a	−73.7	−30.0	−10.0	−0.05	−22.2
Mean Reserve Taste = μ_r	−49.4	−30.0	−13.5	−20.1	−30.0
SD Active Taste = σ_a	54.6	20.1	22.2	33.1	11.0
SD Reserve Taste = σ_r	5.5	4.1	2.7	2.0	16.4
Switch Cost if Leave Active <3 Years	−601.8	−270.4	−221.4	−121.5	−81.5
Switch Cost if Leave Reserve	−445.9	−109.9	−134.3	−298.9	−365.0
Switch Cost if Switch from Civilian to Reserve	−992.3	−735.1	−601.8	−1,339.4	−1,339.4
Personal Discount Factor	0.94	0.92	0.89	0.90	0.91

NOTE: Transformed parameters are denominated in thousands of dollars, with the exception of the personal discount factor.

gists. The relatively large estimated standard deviation of the taste distribution for psychologists is such that 68 percent are in the range of −$73,700 ± $54,600.

Mean taste for reserve duty is also negative across all occupations and ranges from −$13,500 for nurses to −$49,400 for psychologists. The results suggest that for these occupations the mean active taste is about the same size as the mean reserve taste.

Estimates for the standard deviation of reserve taste are all small. This is true even for the large sample of all nurses, so the result is not necessarily a result of the small sample sizes of some of the occupations. By comparison, the scale parameter "within nest" is much larger. As was the case for psychiatrists, these results suggest that movement into and out of the reserve and civilian statuses is largely driven by random shocks rather than diverse tastes among members.

The switching costs for leaving active duty early range from approximately −$81,500 for social workers to −$601,800 for psychologists. The switching costs for leaving both active and reserve duty ("Switch if Leave Reserve") range from −$109,900 to −$445,900. In all cases, the cost of switching back to a reserve component after being a civilian was larger than the other costs, ranging from −$601,800 for nurses to −$1,339,400 for occupational therapists/physician assistants and social workers. As with psychiatrists, very few individuals make this switch in the data.

The personal discount factors range from 0.89 to 0.92 (except for psychologists, for whom we fixed the discount factor at 0.94). These factors imply average personal discount rates of 9 to 14 percent. For comparison, Asch, Hosek, and Mattock (2014) estimate discount factors of 0.933 for Army officers, 0.942 for Navy officers, and 0.941 for Air Force officers, hence a discount rate of about 6 percent. The results for the mental health occupational areas suggest that personnel in these occupations place a somewhat higher value on dollars today versus tomorrow than do officers at large.

Model Fit for Other Mental Health Care Providers

Figures 6.3 through 6.7 show the model fit graphs for active and reserve service, for each occupation. As before, the red lines are simulated cumulative retention and the black lines are retention observed in the data.

We see that many individuals leave active duty after three to four years, which is consistent with a three-year active duty minimum service obligation. Similarly, reserve retention peaks around year eight, suggesting that many individuals complete their eight-year minimum service obligation in the reserve component rather than in the Individual Ready Reserve. The model fits each occupation reasonably well and captures the drop in participation after ADSO is complete as well as the peak in reserve participation.

Summary

For each occupation, we constructed expressions for the probabilities of staying in the current state or transitioning to another and used these to build a likelihood expression for each person's active retention and possible movement into or out of the reserves. The individual likelihoods multiply together to obtain a likelihood expression for the sample, and the sample likelihood was maximized with respect to the taste, shock, switching costs, and discount factor parameters of the DRM. The retention data came from DMDC's Work Experience File for cohorts entering in 1990 to 2000 at O-3 for psychiatrists and psychologists and O-1 for the other occupations. Most parameter estimates are statistically significant, and graphics show a good fit between observed and predicted retention. The estimated DRMs provide a basis for simulating the retention effects of changes in compensation and S&I pays.

Figure 6.3
Model Fit Results: Psychologists

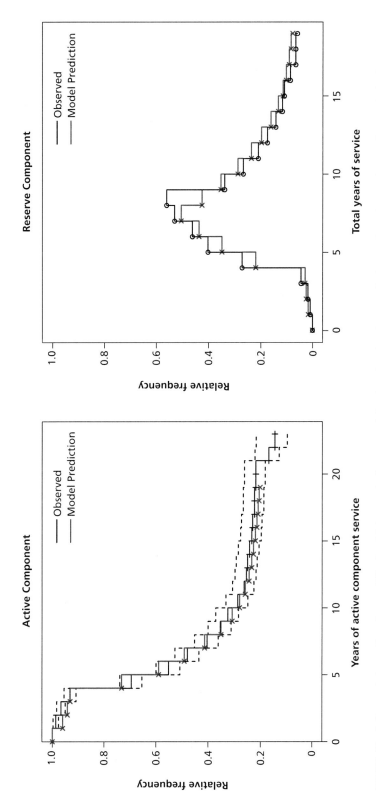

NOTES: The left panel shows the observed Kaplan-Meier survival curve and simulated active duty survival curve based on estimates for psychologists. The panel on the right shows the observed histogram and simulated reserve participation histogram for these psychologists.
RAND *RR1425-6.3*

Figure 6.4
Model Fit Results: Mental Health Nurses

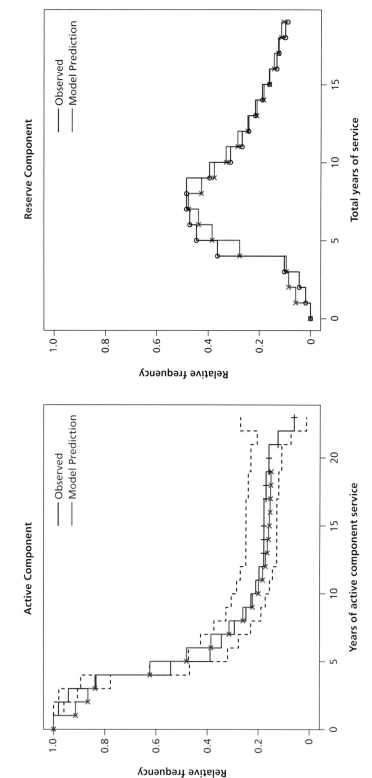

NOTES: The left panel shows the observed Kaplan-Meier survival curve and simulated active duty survival curve based on estimates for mental health nurses. The panel on the right shows the observed histogram and simulated reserve participation histogram for these mental health nurses.

Figure 6.5
Model Fit Results: All Nurses

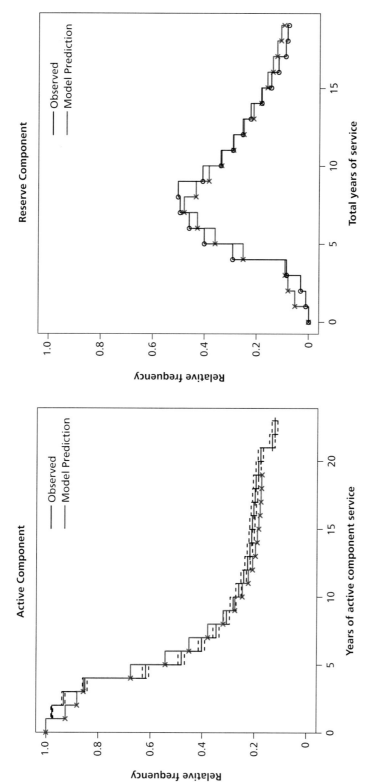

NOTES: The left panel shows the observed Kaplan-Meier survival curve and simulated active duty survival curve based on estimates for all nurses. The panel on the right shows the observed histogram and simulated reserve participation histogram for these nurses.

RAND *RR1425-6.5*

Figure 6.6
Model Fit Results: Occupational Therapists/Physician Assistants

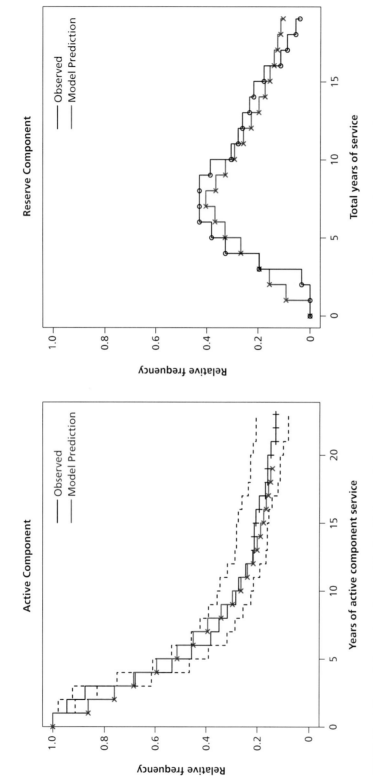

NOTES: The left panel shows the observed Kaplan-Meier survival curve and simulated active duty survival curve based on estimates for occupational therapists and physician assistants. The panel on the right shows the observed histogram and simulated reserve participation histogram for these occupational therapists and physician assistants.

Figure 6.7
Model Fit Results: Social Workers

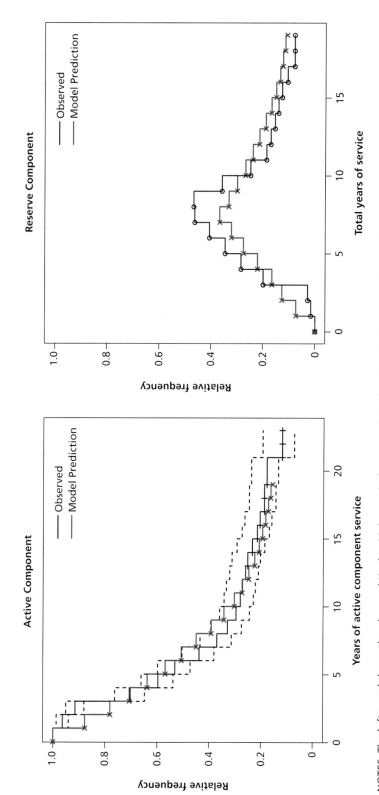

NOTES: The left panel shows the observed Kaplan-Meier survival curve and simulated active duty survival curve based on estimates for social workers. The panel on the right shows the observed histogram and simulated reserve participation histogram for these social workers.

RAND *RR1425-6.7*

CHAPTER SEVEN

Policy Simulations and Analyses

In this chapter, we demonstrate the simulation capability with selected policy examples. For military psychiatrists, the specific policy we consider is a 25 percent increase in MSP values for a two-, three-, and four- year service obligation. For other mental health care provider occupations, the specific policies are recent changes in S&I pay for these occupations, described below. Many of these policies began after the period covered by our data, i.e., after 2010. We present simulation results for each occupation and discuss the S&I pay policy we simulate.

Simulation Results for Psychiatrists

We simulated a 25 percent increase in MSP for each contract length choice relative to 2013 MSP values. Thus, we considered an MSP of $19,550 for a two-year commitment, $32,200 for a three-year commitment, and $49,450 for a four-year commitment. The choice of 25 percent is arbitrary, and other values could have been used.

Figure 7.1 shows the steady-state results of this increase for psychiatrists who received a HPSP, did a four-year military residency, and faced a three- or four-year service obligation. We see no effect on retention during the years of service when members were military residents and meeting their service obligation. That is, we see no retention effect before the completion of YOS 7. The effect at YOS 7 is extremely small, since those with a four-year service obligation are still completing their obligation in this year. The retention effect at YOS 8 is slightly larger, yet the effects on retention are most visible beginning at YOS 9. The overall steady-state effect is a 5.3 percent increase in the number of psychiatrists relative to the baseline. The increase is greatest in YOS 10 to 20 and averages about 20 percent higher than baseline. There is little increase in retention after YOS 20.

Simulation Results for Other Mental Health Care Providers

S&I pays for other mental health professionals have changed since 2009, and Table 7.1 shows the values for 2013. Previously, psychologists, nurses, occupational therapists, physician assistants, and social workers with a post-baccalaureate degree and with certification in their specialties were eligible for Diplomate Pay or BCP. This pay was $2,000 per year to $5,000 per year depending on years of service. Pay regulations published in April 2013 allowed psychologists, physician assistants, and social workers to select between the previous Diplomate Pay/ BCP and a new Health Professional Officers (HPO) BCP of $6,000 per year. In addition,

Figure 7.1
Simulated Retention of a 25 Percent Increase in MSP for
Psychiatrists Who Received HPSP with a Four-Year Military
Residency and Three- or Four-Year Service Obligation

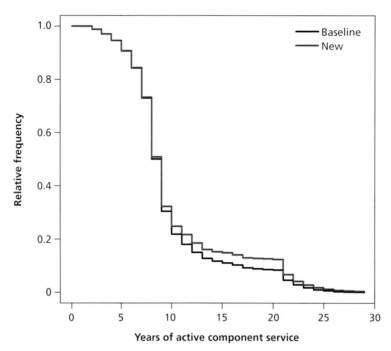

NOTES: Simulated survival curves for psychiatrists who entered through the
HPSP program and who had a three- to four-year ADSO and a four-year
military residency. The baseline survival curve shows the estimated curve
based on the observed data, while the simulated curve estimates the change
in survival for a 25 percent increase in MSP, using the parameter estimates
reported in the previous chapter.
RAND *RR1425-7.1*

fully qualified psychologists and physician assistants became eligible for HPO incentive pay of
$5,000 per year. The HPO Incentive Pay can be taken concurrently with an HPO Retention
Bonus, which is available to psychologists and physician assistants below grade O-7 who have
at least eight years of creditable service or have completed any ADSO associated with their
accession bonus or medical training. The annual amount of the retention bonus ranges from
$10,000 per year for two years to $20,000 per year for four years. Social workers are also eligible for HPO Incentive Pay and Retention Bonus, but the amount was zero as of April 2013
(DoD 7000.14, Vol. 7a). Certain fully qualified nurses, including psychiatric/mental health
nurses, are eligible for ISP of $5,000 per year for a one-year contract to $20,000 per year for a
four-year contract. Psychologists, physician assistants, nurses, and social workers are also eligible for various accession bonuses, though we do not analyze them here.

We simulate the retention effects of offering the HPO Incentive Pay and the HPO Retention Bonus. These pays are zero for social workers. Nonetheless, we assume HPO Incentive
Pay and Retention Bonus for social workers equal to what is available to physician assistants to
demonstrate the capability. For mental health nurses, we show the steady-state effects of offering ISP for specialty nurses.

Table 7.1
New S&I Pays Available to Other Mental Health Providers

Special or Incentive Pay	Eligibility	Amount in 2013	Obligation
Health Professional Officers Board Certified Pay	Psychologist, physician assistant, social worker; certified by professional board (must choose between this and existing board pay)	$6,000/year	1 year
Health Professional Officers Incentive Pay	Psychologist, physician assistant, social worker, completed qualifying training	$5,000/year (psychologist/ physician assistant) $0 (social worker) Can be taken along with HPO retention bonus	1 year
Health Professional Officers Retention Bonus	Psychologist, physician assistant, social worker, below O-7 plus 8 years of creditable service or completed obligation for medical training/accession bonus	$10,000/year for 2 years $15,000/year for 3 years $20,000/year for 4 years For psychologist/physician assistant ($0 for Social Worker)	2–4 years
ISP for specialty nurses	Psychiatric/mental health nurse, completed specialty training	$5,000/year for 1 year $10,000/year for 2 years $15,000/year for 3 years $20,000/year for 4 years	1–4 years

SOURCE: S&I pays available for mental health providers as reported in pay regulations published in 2013.

Figure 7.2 shows the results for psychologists. The graph shows the steady-state effects of offering both HPO Incentive Pay and Retention Bonus. This increases retention among psychologists, especially those with five or more years of service. In our model, psychologists begin to qualify for the incentive pay after four years of service so the larger increase after YOS 4 is expected. However, because personnel are forward looking in the model, retention increases slightly even before YOS 5 as psychologists look ahead and see that the value to staying increases a result of these S&I pays. In the steady state, when all officers have spent their entire career under a policy environment that includes these pays, the force size of psychologists increases by 6.3 percent relative to the baseline. This assumes no increase in the size of the entering cohort; the increase in force size is the result of higher retention.

Figures 7.3 and 7.4 show the respective effects on physician assistant and social worker retention of offering the HPO Incentive Pay and Retention Bonus. In the steady state, we find that physician assistant force size increases by 8.5 percent relative to the baseline, and social worker retention increases by 11.3 percent. Again, in actuality, these S&I pays are zero for social workers as of 2013, but the simulations show the retention effects to demonstrate what would happen should these S&I pays for social workers be positive and equal to what physician assistants get.

Figure 7.5 shows the simulation results for mental health nurses of ISP for specialty nurses. The ISP for specialty nurses is the same size as the HPO Incentive Pay and Retention Bonus, but the retention effect of ISP is larger for nurses than the effect of HPO Incentive Pay and Retention Bonus for psychologists or physician assistants. For mental health nurses, the steady-state force size increases by 15.1 percent. The effect is larger for nurses because their civilian pay opportunities are lower, although military pay is the same for nurses as it is for physician assistants (see Chapter Four).

Figure 7.2
Simulated Psychologist Retention with Health Professional
Officers Incentive Pay and Health Professional Officers Retention
Bonus

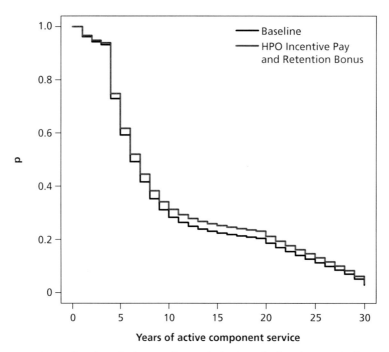

NOTES: Simulated survival curves for psychologists. The baseline survival
curve shows the estimated curve based on the observed data, while the
simulated curve estimates the change in survival given the HPO Incentive
Pay and the HPO Retention Bonus, using the parameter estimates
reported in the previous chapter.
RAND *RR1425-7.2*

Summary

To demonstrate a simulation capability, we simulated the retention effect of a 25 percent increase in MSP for each contract length choice relative to the 2013 MSP values for psychiatrists who had received an HPSP. There was little change in retention during the first eight years of service starting from when the psychiatrist began a military residency. During these years, the psychiatrist completed a four-year residency and then had to fulfill a typically three- or four-year ADSO. Retention increased in YOS 10 to 20 as simulated service members responded to the increase in MSP. Retention after 20 years was only slightly higher than at baseline.

For other mental health professionals, we simulated the retention effects of the HPO Incentive Pay and the HPO Retention Bonus to psychologists, physician assistants, and social workers, and the ISP for specialty nurses to mental health nurses. The simulations showed an increase in retention in response to these incentives. Overall, the simulations offer evidence of the capability to predict the retention effects of changes in S&I pay and other elements of military compensation.

Figure 7.3
Simulated Physician Assistant Retention with Health Professional
Officers Incentive Pay and Health Professional Officers Retention
Bonus

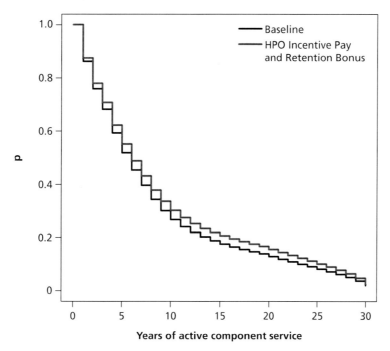

NOTES: Simulated survival curves for physician assistants. The baseline
survival curve shows the estimated curve based on the observed data, while
the simulated curve estimates the change in survival given the HPO Incentive
Pay and the HPO Retention Bonus, using the parameter estimates reported
in the previous chapter.
RAND *RR1425-7.3*

Figure 7.4
Simulated Social Work Retention with Health Professional Officers
Incentive Pay and Health Professional Officers Retention Bonus

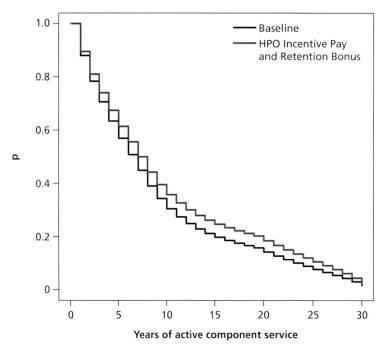

NOTES: Simulated survival curves for social workers. The baseline survival
curve shows the estimated curve based on the observed data, while the
simulated curve estimates the change in survival given the HPO Incentive
Pay and the HPO Retention Bonus, using the parameter estimates reported
in the previous chapter.
RAND *RR1425-7.4*

Figure 7.5
Simulated Mental Health Nurse Retention with the Incentive
Special Pay for Specialty Nurses

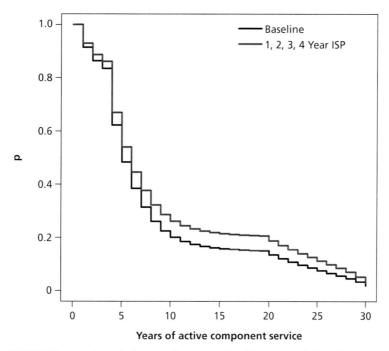

NOTES: Simulated survival curves for mental health nurses. The baseline survival curve shows the estimated curve based on the observed data, while the simulated curve estimates the change in survival given the HPO Incentive Pay and the HPO Retention Bonus, using the parameter estimates reported in the previous chapter.

RAND *RR1425-7.5*

CHAPTER EIGHT

Conclusion

Our research has pursued the objective of creating a capability to predict how retention would be affected by changes in the type or amount of pays for military mental health professionals. We adapted the DRM to mental health occupations and estimated models for psychiatrists, psychologists, nurses, mental health care nurses, occupational therapists along with physician assistants, and social workers. To develop data needed by the DRM for each occupation, we reviewed S&I pays and developed estimates of expected military pay by age; used ACS data to develop estimates of expected civilian pay by age; created DRM code to handle service member choice of the length of obligation under MSP; and obtained longitudinal data on retention. Most parameters of the estimated DRMs were statistically significant, and the model fit the active and reserve retention data well. Finally, we demonstrated the capability of the estimated DRM to simulate the steady-state retention effect of counterfactual changes in S&I pay.

The completed research has made progress toward meeting the project's objective, but there are limitations to keep in mind. The first concerns sample size and the number of years over which service members are followed. The sample included entry cohorts of officers from 1990 through 2000 and followed through 2010. Service members were followed for as long as 21 years and as short as 11 years. In the future, it would be worth updating the file to follow personnel to the latest year available, currently 2015. This would not only produce longer files but also additional cohorts of entrants, thereby expanding the sample size for each specialty. The longer files might improve model fit in years of service past 20, though, as mentioned, the fit is already good. Second, the model does not control for changes in the pace of military operations. Deployments increased substantially in the past decade and have decreased since then. Many service members were exposed to deployment trauma, such as witnessing a death or being involved in close combat. Such exposure is a predictor of PTSD and major depressive disorder symptoms, and hence of the potential demand for mental health care among service members and their families (and for those who leave the military). It may be worth assessing the realized increase in demand and the extent to which S&I pays did, or could, help to retain mental health care providers to meet the demand. Third, although the estimated DRMs and simulation capability can show the effect of S&I pays on retention, other data are needed to track retention, determine when provider supply is inadequate or more than adequate, and trigger S&I pay increases or decreases, respectively. That is, the simulation capability is only one part of a system of information needed to adjust S&I pay. Fourth, changes in S&I pay type, availability, or amount could affect the size and taste of entering cohorts. The estimation assumed that the taste distribution was constant for the entering cohorts from 1990 to 2000. Future work could extend the model to allow for cohort-specific estimation of the taste parameters, sample size permitting. It could also address the effect of S&I pay, particularly the generosity of HPSP and FAP, to attract larger entry cohorts if desired. Similarly, the model could be extended to consider how changes in the pace of military operations affect the retention of these officers.

Cost to the Individual of a Two-Period Commitment

The value function for being in the military for one period and having the choice of continuing in the military in the second period or leaving is

$$V_1^m = \gamma + w_1^m + \beta EMax\left(V_2^m, V_2^n\right) + \varepsilon_1^m,$$

where γ is the individual's value of the "taste" for military service, w_1^m is the period 1 military wage, β is the personal discount factor, *Emax* takes the expected value of the maximum of the value functions for the military and nonmilitary status in period 2 given being in the military in period 1, and ε_1^m is a random shock. The taste represents the monetary value of unobserved, persistent differences between the military and nonmilitary statuses that are specific to the individual.

The value function for the military with a two-period commitment is

$$V(2)_1^m = \gamma + w_1^m + \beta(\gamma + w_2^m + \beta EMax(V_3^m, V_3^n)) + \varepsilon_1^m.$$

The difference between the unconstrained and constrained value functions is

$$V_1^m - V(2)_1^m = \beta EMax\left(V_3^m, V_3^n\right) - \beta\left(\gamma + w_2^m + \beta EMax\left(V_3^m, V_3^n\right)\middle| m\right).$$

The expression can be expanded to

$$p\left(\gamma + w_2^m + \beta EMax\left(V_3^{m|m}, V_3^{n|m}\right)\right) + (1-p)\left(w_2^n + \beta EMax\left(V_3^{m|n}, V_3^{n|n}\right)\right),$$

where $p = \Pr(V_2^m > V_2^n)$. Here, the expression $\gamma + w_2^m + \beta EMax(V_3^{m|m}, V_3^{n|m})$ should be understood as conditional on $V_2^m > V_2^n$. Similarly, $1 - p = \Pr(V_2^n > V_2^m)$, and $w_2^n + \beta EMax(V_3^{m|n}, V_3^{n|n})$ is conditional on $V_2^m < V_2^n$. When $V_2^m > V_2^n$—that is, when $Max(V_2^m, V_2^n) = V_2^m$—the individual chooses to stay in the military in period 2, while when $Max(V_2^m, V_2^n) = V_2^n$, the individual chooses to leave and be nonmilitary. To emphasize the conditionality, we use the notation "$|m$" and "$|n$" in the *EMax* expressions for period 3, indicating that the status chosen in period 2 was military m or nonmilitary n.

Substituting and simplifying,

$$V_1^m - V(2)_1^m = \beta(1-p)\left(w_2^n + \beta EMax\left(V_3^{m|n}, V_3^{n|n} \right) - \left(\gamma + w_2^m + \beta EMax\left(V_3^{m|m}, V_3^{n|m} \right) \right) \right).$$

Here, $w_2^n + \beta EMax\left(V_3^{m|n}, V_3^{n|n} \right)$ is the return from leaving the military in period 2, and $\gamma + w_2^m + \beta EMax\left(V_3^{m|m}, V_3^{n|m} \right)$ is the return from staying in the military in period 2. The difference in these returns is multiplied by $(1-p)$, the probability in period 2 that $V_2^n > V_2^m$. So, the gain from being free to choose whether to stay or leave in the period 2 versus being constrained to stay equals the chance that leaving would have been advantageous ($V_2^n > V_2^m$) times the amount by which it would have been advantageous. Another way of stating the condition is

$$V_1^m - V(2)_1^m = \beta \Pr\left(V_2^n > V_2^m \right)\left(V_2^m - V_2^n \middle| V_2^n > V_2^m \right).$$

By construction, this difference is *positive.* Stating the condition the other way around, the cost of being constrained to stay in period 2 versus being free to choose whether to stay or leave in period 2 is the negative value

$$V(2)_1^m - V_1^m = \beta \Pr\left(V_2^n > V_2^m \right)\left(V_2^m - V_2^n \middle| V_2^n > V_2^m \right).$$

In the DRM, a person cannot reenter the active component military after leaving it, so $Emax(V_3^{m|n}, V_3^{n|n}) = V_3^{n|n}$. This is the present discounted value of civilian earnings from period 3 forward. Under the assumption that this present discounted value is independent of when one left the military, there is no need to condition on "n" in period 2 and we can write $Emax(V_3^{n|n}) = V_3^n$. Similarly, if the individual cannot reenter the military, it is not necessary to use the notation "$|m$" in $EMax(V_3^{m|m}, V_3^{n|m}) = V_3^n$ provided that it is understood that this choice can arise only if the individual stayed in the military in the previous period. Using these assumptions and simplified notation, the gain from being free to choose whether to stay or leave in the second period versus being constrained to stay in period 2 is

$$V_1^m - V(2)_1^m = \beta(1-p)\left(w_2^n + \beta V_3^n \right) - \left(\gamma + w_2^m + \beta EMax\left(V_3^m, V_3^n \right) \right).$$

The shocks to the military and nonmilitary alternatives in any period are assumed to have an extreme value distribution with a mode of zero and a scale of lambda: $\varepsilon\text{-}EV[0,\lambda]$. With an extreme value shock, the quantity $a + \varepsilon$ is distributed as $EV[a,\lambda]$. The mean of this distribution equals the scale factor times Euler's gamma plus the mode $\phi\lambda + a$, where $\phi \approx 0.577$. If the mode is transformed by subtracting $\phi\lambda$, then $a - \phi\lambda + \varepsilon$ is distributed as $EV[a - \phi\lambda, \lambda]$, with a mean of a. Also, if two quantities V^m and V^n have the form $a + \varepsilon$ and we subtract $\phi\lambda$ from each, their maximum has an extreme value distribution, namely,

$$Max\left(V^m, V^n \right) \sim EV\left[\lambda \ln\left(e^{V^m / \lambda} + e^{V^n / \lambda} \right) - \phi\lambda, \lambda \right].$$

The mean of this distribution is $\lambda\ln\left(e^{V^m/\lambda}+e^{V^n/\lambda}\right)$. With extreme value shocks, the probability that $V^m > V^n$ has the form

$$\Pr(V^m > V^n) = \frac{e^{V^m}}{e^{V^m}+e^{V^n}}.$$

Therefore, in the DRM the expected net loss from being constrained to stay in the military in period 2 rather than having the choice to stay or to leave is

$$V_1^m - V(2)_1^m = \beta\frac{e^{V_2^m}}{e^{V_2^m}+e^{V_2^n}}\left(w_2^n + \beta\lambda\ln\left(e^{V_3^m|n/\lambda}+e^{V_3^n|n/\lambda}\right)-\left(\gamma+w_2^m+\beta\lambda\ln\left(e^{V_3^m|m/\lambda}+e^{V_3^n|m/\lambda}\right)\right)\right)$$

That is, if the cost to an individual of a constrained contract is $V_1^m - V(2)_1^m$, then offering compensation equal to this cost would leave the individual indifferent. Thus, this also represents the amount needed make an individual with taste γ indifferent between accepting a contract with a two-period commitment versus one with a one-period commitment. Imposing the rule that the individual cannot reenter the military, using the assumption that the present discounted value of the nonmilitary path in a given period is independent of when one left the military, and using the simplified notation, the cost is

$$V_1^m - V(2)_1^m = \beta\frac{e^{V_2^n}}{e^{V_2^m}+e^{V_2^n}}\left(w_2^n + \beta V_3^n - \left(\gamma+w_2^m+\beta\lambda\ln\left(e^{\frac{V_3^m}{\lambda}}+e^{\frac{V_3^n}{\lambda}}\right)\right)\right)$$

$$= \beta(1-p)\left(w_2^n + \beta V_3^n - \left(\gamma+w_2^m+\beta\lambda\ln\left(e^{\frac{V_3^m}{\lambda}}+e^{\frac{V_3^n}{\lambda}}\right)\right)\right)$$

By implication, the amount needed to compensate for a constrained contract, such as a multiyear commitment, is positively related to the personal discount factor β and the probability that $V_2^n > V_2^m$. This depends positively on the current nonmilitary wage and the present discounted value of future nonmilitary earnings, and negatively on the taste for military service, current military wage, and the value of continuing in the military for another period, recognizing that one can choose to stay or leave at the end of that period. The taste for military service can be positive or negative. If taste is negative, the amount needed to compensate for a multiyear commitment is higher. More generally, the analysis indicates that the more attractive the military career relative to the nonmilitary career on an ongoing basis, the lower the cost to the individual of a multiyear contract.

Possible Selectivity by Military Financial Aid Pathway

Table 3.1 in Chapter Three summarized information about the types of financial aid with respect to the cost of medical school and briefly discussed how to incorporate the choice of military financial aid into the DRM. Here, we provide a more formal treatment.

For an informed, foresighted individual, the choice of military financial aid involves a selection of the type of aid and, for HPSP and FAP, the amount of aid. The *choice set* is {none; USUHS; two-, three-, or four-year HPSP and a military or civilian residency program (four years in psychiatry); two- or three-year HPSP, internship, and a two- or three-year GMO tour (Navy); two-, three-, or four-year FAP; ADHPLRP}. The individual will choose the alternative with the highest value.

Table B.1 has value functions by type of military financial aid, starting the clock at the outset of the residency program. The table shows the cost of medical school in an approximate form and without discounting in the medical school years. For instance, four years of medical school tuition and living expense appear as $4(T + L)$. The value functions for USUHS, FAP, and a two- or three-year HPSP plus internship and GMO tour are correct as shown in Table B.1, but the value functions for HPSP paths are somewhat more complicated.

In particular, an HPSP recipient must apply to a military residency program and might be granted a waiver to attend a civilian residency program. Also, an HPSP recipient might want a military residency but none might be available, so this person would have to do a civilian residency. Let q be the probability that a military residency is available to the individual, and let s be the probability that permission for a civilian residency is granted.[1] The probabilities of the various pathways are

- Prefer and obtain a military residency: $\Pr(V^{HPSP,\ mil\ res} > V^{HPSP,\ mil\ res})q$
- Prefer but not obtain a military residency: $\Pr(V^{HPSP,\ mil\ res} > V^{HPSP,\ mil\ res})(1 - q)$
- Prefer and obtain a civilian residency: $\Pr(V^{HPSP,\ mil\ res} > V^{HPSP,\ mil\ res})s$
- Prefer but not obtain a civilian residency: $\Pr(V^{HPSP,\ mil\ res} > V^{HPSP,\ mil\ res})(1 - s)$.

The values of q and s are not known in the data and add uncertainty to the HPSP that will be realized. The path may be the individual's first choice or second choice.

To get a feel for the alternative pathways, we will consider four cases: a four-year HPSP versus a three-year HPSP, both with a military residency; a four-year HPSP with a military versus a civilian residency; a four-year FAP versus a four-year HPSP for a person wanting a

---

[1] Assume that if a military residency is not available, a civilian residency can be obtained with probability one. Assume that if permission for a civilian residency is not granted, a military residency can be obtained with probability one.

Table B.1
Value Functions by Type of Military Financial Aid for Medical Education, as of Start of Residency Program: Psychiatrists

Type	Net Medical School Cost and Subsequent Returns[a]
FAP[b]	$-(4-y)(T+L) + \sum_{t=1}^{4}\beta^{t-1}w_t^n + \sum_{t=5}^{ADSO}\beta^{t-1}(w_t^{m,O\text{-}3}+\gamma) + \beta^{ADSO}EMax(V_{ADSO+1}^{m|n}, V_{ADSO+1}^{n|n})$
HPSP, civilian residency[c]	$-(4-y)(T+L) + \sum_{t=1}^{4}\beta^{t-1}w_t^n + \sum_{t=5}^{ADSO}\beta^{t-1}(w_t^{m,O\text{-}3}+\gamma) + \beta^{ADSO}EMax(V_{ADSO+1}^{m|n}, V_{ADSO+1}^{n|n})$
HPSP, military residency[d]	$-(4-y)(T+L) + \sum_{t=1}^{4}\beta^{t-1}(w_t^{m,O\text{-}3}+\gamma) + \sum_{t=5}^{ADSO}\beta^{t-1}(w_t^{m,O\text{-}3}+\gamma) + \beta^{ADSO}EMax(V_{ADSO+1}^{m|m}, V_{ADSO+1}^{n|m})$
2-year HPSP, military internship, 2-year GMO[e]	$-2(T+L) + \sum_{t=1}^{3}\beta^{t-1}(w_t^{m,O\text{-}3}+\gamma) + \beta^3 EMax(V_4^m, V_4^n)$
USUHS[f]	$4(\overline{w}^{m,O\text{-}3}+\gamma-L) + \sum_{t=1}^{4}\beta^{t-1}(w_t^{m,O\text{-}3}+\gamma) + \sum_{t=5}^{11}\beta^{t-1}(w_t^{m,O\text{-}3,4}+\gamma) + \beta^{11}EMax(V_{12}^{m|m}, V_{12}^{n|m})$
None	$-4(T+L) + \sum_{t=1}^{4}\beta^{t-1}w_t^n + \sum_{t=5}^{60}\beta^{t-1}w_t^n$

a γ is the individual's taste for military service.

b The FAP ADSO is a minimum of two years in the Army and up to four years depending on the amount of financial assistance sought, and a minimum of three years in the Navy and Air Force and up to five years. "y" refers to the number of years of financial aid. "|n" refers to the residency program being civilian (nonmilitary).

c For a civilian residency, the HPSP ADSO is a minimum of two years and up to four years. Also, the function takes the civilian residency as given, but in fact an HPSP recipient must apply for a military residency and might or might not be granted a waiver for a civilian residency. See text.

d A military residency (and internship) takes four years and incurs an ADSO of three years.

e After the GMO tour, the individual can leave the military and do a civilian residency, or stay and do a military residency. For a three-year HPSP and three-year GMO tour, the cost and returns are $-(T+L)-\sum_{t=5}^{8}\beta^{t-1}w_t^{m,O\text{-}1}+\beta^8 EMax(V_9^m, V_9^n)$.

f $\overline{w}^{m,O\text{-}1}$ is the average of military pay at the O-1 level over four years of USUHS medical school. Also, the expression assumes no tour of duty before residency.

civilian residency but unsure of obtaining one; and USUHS versus a four-year HPSP with a military residency.

Case 1. Four-year versus three-year HPSP both with a military residency. A four-year HPSP is preferred if the additional year's worth of medical school tuition and living expense paid by the HPSP is greater than the discounted expected cost of being obligated to another year of service. The latter equals the probability of finding a civilian position that pays more than the military times the difference between civilian salary and military pay plus taste (i.e., the intrinsic value of service in the military):

$$T + L - \beta^7 \Pr\left(w_8^c > w_8^{m,0\text{-}3} \right)\left(w_8^c - \left(w_8^{m,0\text{-}3} + \gamma \right) \right) + \beta^8 \left(EMax\left(V_9^{m|m}, V_9^{n|m} \right) - EMax\left(V_9^{m|n}, V_9^{n|n} \right) \right) > 0$$

It follows that the preference for a four-year HPSP over a three-year HPSP increases with taste for the military. Also, the expression in parentheses on the right is the difference in the value of the choice in year 9 given a military residency versus a civilian residency, and this difference is probably negligible.

If so, and to relate this to the foregoing discussion, median out-of-pocket costs $(T + L)$ for attending medical school in 2013–2014 were \$58,000 to \$77,000, so for illustration suppose costs were \$67,000. A person might have completed medical school at age 26, a psychiatry residency at age 30, and be 34 years old at "year 8," giving a predicted civilian wage of about \$180,000 (Figure 5.1). RMC for an O-3 with eight years of service in 2014 was \$93,000, and we assume \$12,000 VSP and \$15,000 ASP are added to that for a total of \$120,000. Thus, $w_8^c - w_8^{m,0\text{-}3} = \$60,000$. In Chapter Six we estimate $\beta \approx 0.94$, so $\beta^7 = 0.65$. Because the civilian wage is so much higher than military pay, and because a civilian job offer can very likely be obtained (e.g., when searching in the military during year 7), it is reasonable to assume that $\Pr\left(w_8^c > w_8^{m,0\text{-}3} \right) \approx 1$. So, a four-year HPSP is preferred if \$67,000 – 0.65(\$60,000 – γ) > 0, or if $\gamma > \$60,000 - (\frac{1}{0.65})\$67,000 \approx -\$43,000$. Using $T + L$ of \$58,000 instead of \$67,000 produces a value of –\$29,000, and $T + L$ of \$77,000 gives a value of –\$59,000. This range suggests that a four-year HPSP would be on average more attractive to those attending a high-cost medical school; the threshold is lower so a higher fraction of these students would have tastes greater than the threshold.

Case 2. Four-year HPSP with a military versus a civilian residency. If the individual can get the type of residency desired (assume $q = 1$ and $s = 1$), the military residency is preferred if $V^{HPSP,\, mil\, res} > V^{HPSP,\, mil\, res}$. This condition simplifies to

$$\sum_{t=1}^{4} \beta^{t-1}(w_t^{m,O\text{-}3} + \gamma - w_t^n) + \beta^8 \left(EMax(V_9^{m|m}, V_9^{n|m}) - EMax(V_9^{m|n}, V_9^{n|m}) \right) > 0 .$$

Again assume the rightmost expression is negligible. Then the military residency is preferred if during the residency military pay plus taste exceeds civilian pay:

$$\sum_{t=1}^{4} \beta^{t-1}(w_t^{m,O\text{-}3} + \gamma - w_t^n) > 0 .$$

We saw that military residency pay is about \$20,000 per year higher than civilian residency pay: $w_t^{m,\text{O-}3} - w_t^n \approx \$20,000$. Therefore, this condition is fulfilled if the taste for military service is greater than –\$20,000. A civilian residency is preferred if taste is less than this.

Case 3. Four-year FAP versus four-year HPSP for a person wanting a civilian residency but unsure of obtaining one. The HPSP has a probability s of a civilian residency, while the FAP involves a civilian residency for certain. The four-year FAP ADSO is four years in the Army and five years in the Navy and Air Force; this example assumes a four-year ADSO. The four-year HPSP ADSO is four years. The FAP is preferred if

$$-4(T-A)+(1-s)\sum_{t=1}^{4}\beta^{t-1}(w_t^n-(w_t^{m,\text{O-}3}+\gamma))+(1-s)\beta^8\left(EMax(V_9^{m|n},V_9^{n|n})-EMax(V_9^{m|m},V_9^{n|m})\right)>0$$

Here, $(T-A)$ is tuition and fees minus the FAP annual award. The second term is the difference in compensation between the civilian and military residencies times the probability the individual cannot obtain the civilian residency under the HPSP. Military residency pay exceeds civilian residency pay, so this term will be negative unless taste for the military is sufficiently negative. The second term will be larger in magnitude the smaller is the chance of getting a civilian residency.[2] There is no term for the ADSO years 5 through 8 because this is obligatory military service for both paths, and we assume assignments during this period are not conditioned on whether a military or civilian residency was done. Thus, the FAP-HPSP difference in career value in years 5 to 8 is zero. The rightmost term does allow for different career value depending on the residency, but we suspect that this term will be negligible. If so, the choice between FAP and HPSP simplifies to

$$-4(T-A)+(1-s)\sum_{t=1}^{4}\beta^{t-1}(w_t^n-(w_t^{m,\text{O-}3}+\gamma))>0 \;.$$

The first term is positive for anyone attending a medical school where the FAP annual award A, now \$45,000, exceeds tuition and fees. This is the case for students paying in-state tuition at a public medical school where tuition, fees, and health insurance now average \$33,220. This will not be the case for students paying out-of-state tuition at those schools or for students at private medical schools—tuition and fees are over \$50,000 at those schools. If tuition and fees were \$55,000, then $-4(T-A) = -\$40,000$. The second term will be negative, given that military residency pay is about \$20,000 higher than civilian residency pay, unless the taste for military service is less than –\$20,000. Further, the weight on the second term depends on the chance of a waiver to do a civilian residency. If the chance is high, the individual risks little by accepting the HPSP and the weight on the second term, $(1-s)$, is low. Putting these points together, FAP will tend to be preferred by those attending a low-cost medical school, perceiving a low chance of doing a civilian residency under the HPSP route, and having distaste for the military.

Case 4. USUHS versus a four-year HPSP with a military residency. USUHS provides four years of tuition and fees and pays the medical student as an O-1. Because USUHS has

---

[2] In the case of psychiatry, Mundell's (2010) data suggests that about half of the military psychiatrists had a civilian residency. Some of them might have taken the FAP route, and all of these would have a civilian residency; others were HPSP scholars and had a civilian residency. Because of this mixing, the data do not identify the probability s.

an ADSO of seven years beginning after completion of the residency, it has the highest lock-in cost. The lock-in cost occurs because in each year of obligated service there is a chance of an external offer better than the value of continuing in the military, but the offer cannot be taken because of the obligation (Appendix A). Helping to offset the lock-in cost, O-1 RMC is currently over $50,000 per year, which is about the cost of tuition and fees at a private medical school. Considering free tuition plus the $50,000 salary, USUHS pays roughly twice the amount of HPSP or FAP. In terms of the financial aid shown in Table 5.1, HPSP and FAP stipends are enough to pay medical school living costs L, while USUHS pays approximately $2L$. Using this approximation, USUHS is preferred to a four-year HPSP with a military residency if

$$4(L+\gamma)+\sum_{t=9}^{11}\beta^{t-1}(w_t^{m,\text{O-3,4}}+\gamma)+\beta^{11}EMax(V_{12}^{m|m},V_{12}^{n|m})-\beta^8 EMax(V_9^{m|m},V_9^{n|m})>0.$$

The second and third terms together reflect the locked-in path of staying in the military from YOS 9 through YOS 11 and then being at liberty to choose whether to stay or leave. The fourth term (rightmost) reflects being at liberty to choose whether to stay or leave at YOS 9. Because the individual can choose the better option, this term is greater than or equal to the second and third terms. It is equal only if the expected value of staying is greater than the expected value of leaving in all years, 9, 10, and 11. Therefore, in general the second, third, and fourth terms sum to a value that is zero or negative. Also, this value will be higher (nearer zero coming from the negative direction) the higher the taste for military service and, as Appendix A shows, the higher the military wage compared with the nonmilitary wage. The first term $4(L + \gamma)$ may be of either sign; it will be positive if the taste for military service is positive or not too negative (not less than $-L$). Considering the first term, and the combined second, third, and fourth terms, USUHS is more likely to be preferred to a four-year HPSP with a military residency by individuals with a high taste for military service and higher military pay relative to nonmilitary pay.

Summarizing, these cases exemplify selection on taste that can be induced by different financial pathways into the military. Our sample of psychiatrists is not large enough to test for fine-grained selectivity, but we probe for selectivity in when estimating the model (Chapter Six), finding evidence of higher taste among USUHS graduates than among HPSP graduates.

Reserve Duty Earnings

We estimated basic monthly reserve pay in each YOS by taking an average of basic pay for that YOS, weighted by the number of reserve officers in each grade in that YOS, taken from the FY 2009 Official Guard and Reserve Manpower Strength and Statistics. In keeping with the convention we used for active duty pay, we used only the distribution of reserve officers from grades O-3 to O-7.[1]

Annual reserve earnings were estimated by considering the following pay elements:

- *Weekend drill pay.* We calculated daily reserve earnings from drilling by dividing monthly active duty basic pay by 30. We then multiplied this daily rate by 4 (assuming 4 drills per month) and by 12 (for 12 months of reserve service) to arrive at an annual figure.
- *Active Duty for Training pay (ACDUTRA).* Reservists are typically on active duty for 14 days per year. During this time, they earn prorated basic pay, BAH, and BAS. As discussed above, we calculated daily basic pay by dividing monthly active duty basic pay by 30. Similarly, we calculated daily BAS by dividing monthly BAS rates for officers by 30. We calculated daily BAH as an average of married and single monthly, nonlocality BAH rates. BAS rates and percentage of married officers were taken from the 2009 Green Book (U.S. Department of Defense, Office of the Under Secretary of Defense for Personnel and Readiness, 2009). BAH rates were taken from the website of the Office of the Secretary of Defense. The sum of daily basic pay, BAS, and BAH was then multiplied by 14 to arrive at total annual ACDUTRA pay.
- *Special Pay for Medical Officers.* Medical officers on reserve earn $450 per month (prorated for periods of less than one month) for active duty for annual training, active duty for training, or active duty for special work. We divided $450 by 30 to calculate the daily rate for this pay, then multiplied by 14 to arrive at the annual bonus for training.
- *Tax Advantage.* We assumed that the 6.5 percent tax advantage calculated for active duty medical officers also applied to the reserves. The tax advantage was calculated by multiplying the sum of drill pay, ACDUTRA, and special pay by 0.065.

Each of the components listed above was estimated separately for each of grades O-3 through O-7, and added up to arrive at total reserve pay for that grade. We then estimated annual reserve pay in each YOS by taking an average of annual pay for that YOS, weighted by the number of reserve officers in each grade in that YOS.

---

[1] We also used this approach in Mattock, Hosek, and Asch (2012) and Asch, Hosek, and Mattock (2014).

APPENDIX D

Comparisons of Military Pay Using the Pay Table Approach Versus Observed Pay from the Pay Files

Physicians

We examined the extent to which our assumed military pay line for physicians was similar to the pay actually observed among the cohorts of interest, using DMDC active duty pay files from 1993 to 2009. Our maintained assumption is that our assumed pay line is a better basis for estimating the DRM than is the actual change in pay over time. This assumes that officers making retention decisions in the 1990s and early 2000s would not have fully anticipated the growth in real military compensation after the September 11, 2001, attacks,[1] and that we are actually modeling the expectations of future military and civilian pay growth over a career. To examine actual military pay and its growth over time, we tracked psychiatrist earnings by active duty YOS starting when they were first observed at O-3. To facilitate comparison with the 2009 pay table data used to construct the military pay lines in Chapter Four, all pays are adjusted to 2009 dollars using the Consumer Price Index (CPI).

Figure D.1 shows median psychiatrist compensation, by YOS, in 2009 dollars, for cohorts entering in 1990 to 2000. Basic, RMC, and total pay all increase steadily with YOS. The increase reflects changes in pay by YOS, for instance through promotion, as well as increases in pay schedules over time that outpaced consumer price inflation.

To investigate the contribution of real pay growth over time, we examined median compensation by calendar year using the DMDC pay files. In this case, we did not limit our analysis to the 1990–2000 cohorts, as few members of these cohorts would be on active duty in later years. Instead, we identified all Army physicians in the pay files from 1993 to 2009.[2]

Median basic pay (in 2009 dollars) rose by nearly $15,000, from approximately $56,000 in 1993 to $70,500 by 2009 (Figure D.2). RMC increased by about $25,000, while total pay, including all incentives, rose by $31,000, from $108,000 to $139,000, a 29 percent increase.

How does the active duty pay received compare with our pay line shown in Figure 4.3? Figure D.3 compares median actual pay with our pay line total pay. Similar comparisons, though not shown, for basic pay and RMC give the same result. Our total pay line is based on the 2009 pay tables with S&I pays constructed, as discussed in Chapter Four. As seen, actual pay (labeled "1990–2000 cohorts") increases faster than does our pay line (labeled "Pay tables") for some years of service. Again, the faster increase reflects the gains in real pay over the past decade.

---

[1] More specifically, military pay growth lagged civilian pay growth in the latter half of the 1990s. Basic pay was adjusted upward in 2000 in legislation that also provided for annual increases 0.5 percentage point higher than the usual adjustment over the next six years. In addition, the housing allowance was increased to cover the full, expected cost of adequate housing, not 85 percent of it, which had been the prior guideline. Higher-than-usual basic pay increases continued through 2011.

[2] We focused on Army physicians because the occupation codes are the simplest to identify in this service.

Figure D.1
Median Psychiatrist Compensation by Years of Active Duty Service, 1990–2000 Cohorts (2009 $)

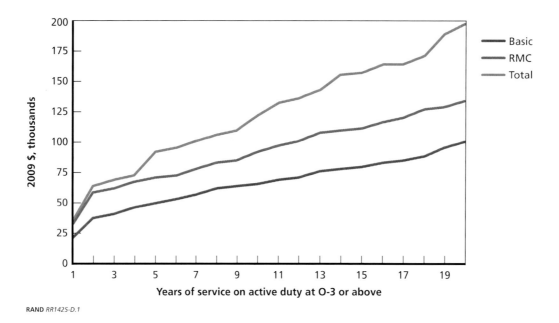

RAND *RR1425-D.1*

Figure D.2
Median Compensation by Calendar Year, Army Nonresident Physicians (2009 $)

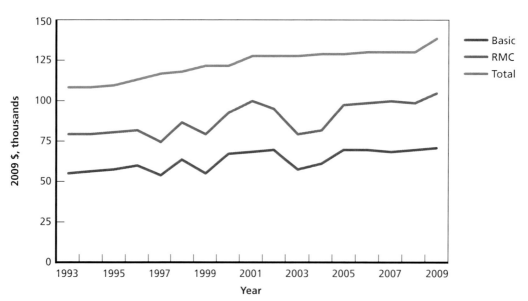

RAND *RR1425-D.2*

Figure D.3
Median Total Pay by Years of Active Duty Service Compared with 2009 Pay Table (2009 $)

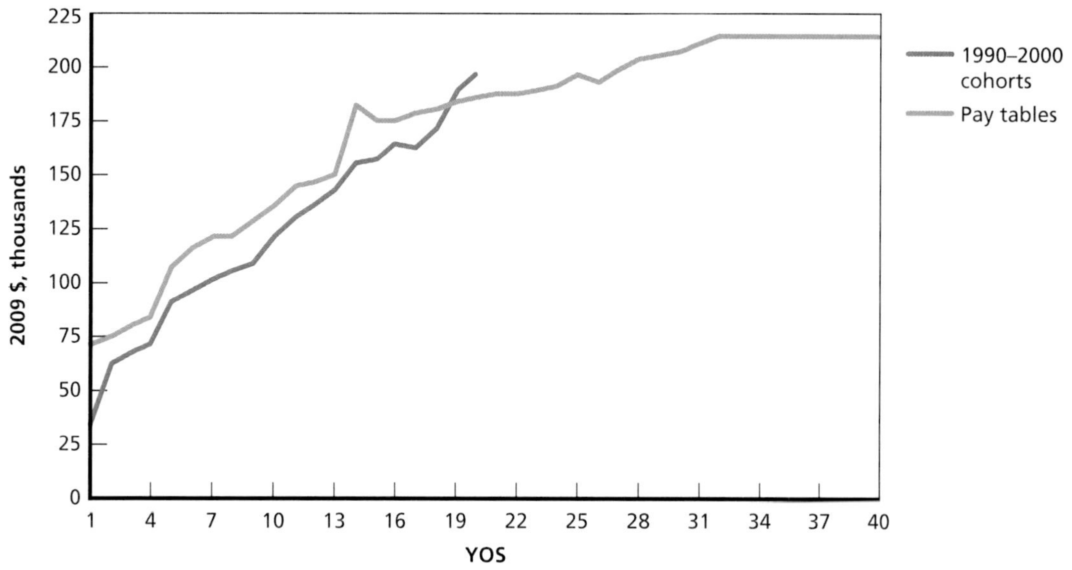

Psychologists

We also examined basic, RMC, and total pay for the 1990–2000 cohorts of psychologists, using the active duty pay files (Figure D.4). We limited our analysis of observed pay in the pay files to psychologists with 20 YOS or fewer, as there are very few psychologists with more than 20 YOS in the 1990–1994 cohorts. The observed pay line from the pay files is somewhat lower than the published, 2009 pay line for each YOS using the pay table approach. Because most psychologists appear to be direct accessions that are first observed on active duty at grade O-3, the reason for this discrepancy is unlikely to be due to internships. Rather, the rise in the real value of basic pay over time (Figure D.5) may explain why the 1990–2000 cohorts received lower pay in their earlier YOS. In particular, basic pay, RMC, and total pay rose considerably faster than the cost of living from 2000 to 2010, pushing the 2009 pay table line up relative to the inflation-adjusted line for the 1990–2000 cohorts.

Other Mental Health Providers

We also calculated basic, RMC, and total pay for the 1990–2000 cohorts of each of these occupations, using the active duty pay files (Figure D.6). As with psychologists, we limited our analysis to officers with 20 YOS or fewer. The actual pay received is similar across these occupations. For each YOS, the actual pay line is somewhat lower than the pay line constructed from the 2009 pay tables, potentially due to the rise in the real value of basic pay over time (Figure D.7).

Figure D.4
Median Total Pay for Psychologists by Years of Active Duty Service Compared with 2009 Pay Table
(2009 $)

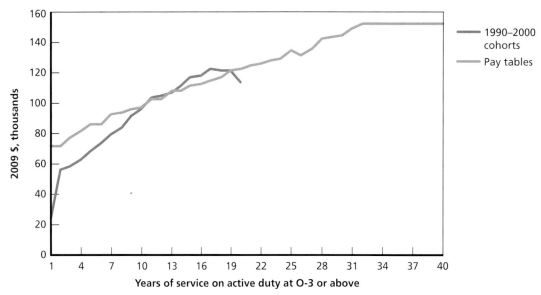

Figure D.5
Median Basic, RMC, and Total Pay for Psychologists by Year (2009 $)

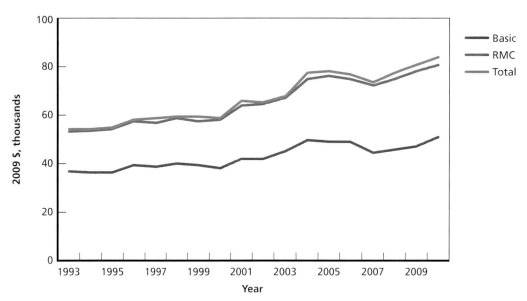

Figure D.6
Median Total Pay for Other Mental Health Providers by Years of Active Duty Service Compared with 2009 Pay Table (2009 $)

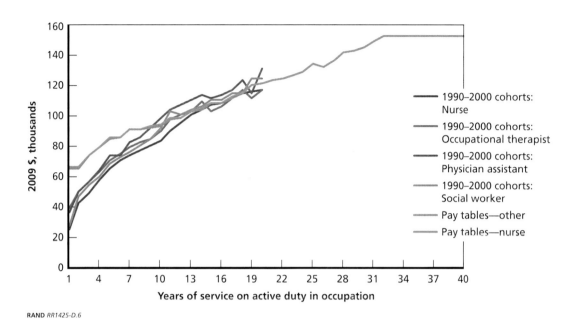

RAND *RR1425-D.6*

Figure D.7
Median Total Pay for Other Mental Health Providers by Year (2009 $)

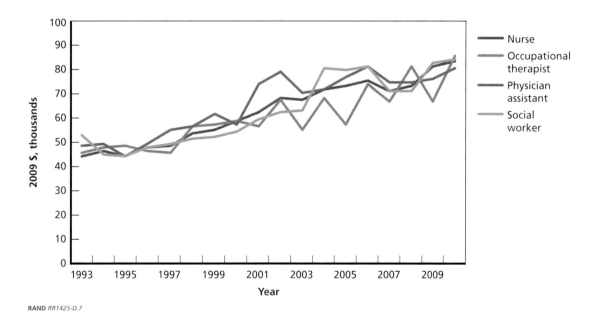

RAND *RR1425-D.7*

Civilian Earnings of Mental Health Care Providers

Table E.1 contains the means and standard deviations by occupation of the variables used in the regression analysis. Table E.2 presents estimates for the right-censored Tobit regressions by occupation, where censoring occurs at the top-code threshold for the dependent variable, annual wage, and salary income. The occupations include physicians, psychologists, registered nurses, physician assistants, occupational therapists, and social workers. For comparison, we also present parallel data and regression estimates for non–mental health care workers.

Table E.1
American Community Survey Sample Means and Standard Deviations

	Physicians		Psychologists		Registered Nurses		Physician Assistants	
	Mean	St. Dev.	Mean	St. Dev.	Mean	St. Dev.	Mean	St. Dev.
Real income (2013 $)	148,985	78,594	72,523	37,838	75,016	32,548	88,796	41,059
Age	45.2	11.6	45.9	12.2	44.8	11.1	40.3	10.9
Female	0.299	0.467	0.590	0.506	0.880	0.328	0.559	0.503
More than 4 years of college	0.988	0.112	0.935	0.254	0.261	0.443	0.557	0.503
2002	0.086	0.285	0.085	0.287	0.085	0.281	0.069	0.256
2003	0.087	0.288	0.082	0.283	0.083	0.278	0.073	0.264
2004	0.089	0.291	0.088	0.291	0.087	0.284	0.082	0.278
2005	0.090	0.292	0.084	0.285	0.093	0.293	0.092	0.293
2006	0.093	0.295	0.084	0.285	0.093	0.294	0.089	0.289
2007	0.105	0.313	0.110	0.321	0.105	0.309	0.094	0.296
2008	0.109	0.318	0.112	0.325	0.106	0.311	0.109	0.316
2009	0.111	0.321	0.116	0.330	0.110	0.316	0.127	0.337
2010	0.114	0.325	0.121	0.335	0.116	0.323	0.135	0.346
2011	0.115	0.325	0.119	0.334	0.122	0.330	0.130	0.341
Veteran 1990 to 2001	0.024	0.156	0.009	0.096	0.017	0.132	0.044	0.208
Veteran 2001 to 2012	0.021	0.146	0.008	0.092	0.013	0.116	0.034	0.184

Table E.1 (continued)

	Occupational Therapists		Social Workers		Non–Mental Health	
	Mean	St. Dev.	Mean	St. Dev.	Mean	St. Dev.
Real Income (2013$)	69,551	24,149	48,282	19,336	79,743	52,376
Age	39.0	10.5	41.5	11.8	42.6	11.6
Female	0.839	0.371	0.780	0.418	0.405	0.496
More than 4 years of college	0.427	0.499	0.413	0.496	0.343	0.480
2002	0.088	0.285	0.081	0.276	0.086	0.284
2003	0.105	0.310	0.084	0.280	0.089	0.287
2004	0.081	0.275	0.087	0.284	0.090	0.290
2005	0.080	0.274	0.091	0.290	0.093	0.293
2006	0.081	0.275	0.099	0.301	0.096	0.298
2007	0.115	0.321	0.107	0.311	0.108	0.314
2008	0.101	0.304	0.110	0.315	0.107	0.312
2009	0.102	0.305	0.111	0.316	0.107	0.312
2010	0.113	0.320	0.114	0.321	0.109	0.316
2011	0.135	0.345	0.116	0.323	0.114	0.322
Veteran 1990 to 2001	0.006	0.079	0.011	0.104	0.017	0.132
Veteran 2001 to 2012	0.004	0.062	0.006	0.079	0.011	0.105

Table E.2
Tobit Regressions of Annual Earnings

	Physicians			Psychologists			Registered Nurses		
	Estimate	St. Error	t Value	Estimate	St. Error	t Value	Estimate	St. Error	t Value
Age	0.2107	0.0031	67.80	0.0628	0.0057	11.02	0.0506	0.0015	32.96
Age-squared	−0.0019	0.0000	−56.68	−0.0006	0.0001	−9.22	−0.0005	0.0000	−28.73
Female	−0.2905	0.0119	−24.37	−0.1078	0.0176	−6.13	−0.1243	0.0075	−16.53
More than 4 years of college	0.0195	0.0431	0.45	0.2171	0.0319	6.81	0.1499	0.0049	30.48
2003	0.0312	0.0335	0.93	0.0938	0.0566	1.66	0.0250	0.0130	1.93
2004	0.0707	0.0272	2.60	0.0764	0.0545	1.40	0.0164	0.0113	1.45
2005	−0.0043	0.0253	−0.17	0.1078	0.0519	2.08	0.0187	0.0111	1.68
2006	0.0410	0.0248	1.65	0.0548	0.0532	1.03	0.0375	0.0110	3.40
2007	0.0326	0.0240	1.36	0.0830	0.0509	1.63	0.0295	0.0111	2.67
2008	0.0913	0.0241	3.79	0.0925	0.0504	1.84	0.0699	0.0109	6.39
2009	0.1015	0.0244	4.17	0.1094	0.0508	2.16	0.0717	0.0109	6.57
2010	0.0583	0.0249	2.34	0.0908	0.0510	1.78	0.0530	0.0113	4.71
2011	0.0988	0.0245	4.03	0.0644	0.0512	1.26	0.0448	0.0112	3.99
Veteran	0.0336	0.0268	1.26	0.0451	0.0377	1.19	−0.0081	0.0143	−0.57
Veteran 1990 to 2001	0.0197	0.0423	0.47	−0.0286	0.1030	−0.28	0.0347	0.0198	1.76
Veteran 2001 to 2012	−0.0570	0.0379	−1.51	0.1300	0.0894	1.45	0.0482	0.0259	1.86
Threshold 2	−0.0254	0.0169	−1.50	0.0501	0.0259	1.94	0.0420	0.0059	7.08
Threshold 3	−0.0093	0.0196	−0.48	0.0699	0.0333	2.10	0.0508	0.0076	6.65
Threshold 4	−0.0216	0.0173	−1.25	0.1691	0.0259	6.52	0.1871	0.0069	27.02
Threshold 5	−0.0688	0.0178	−3.85	0.1847	0.0287	6.43	0.1777	0.0075	23.79
Threshold 6	−0.0487	0.0348	−1.40	0.2892	0.0528	5.47	0.2194	0.0165	13.29
Threshold 7	−0.0935	0.0533	−1.76	0.2928	0.0673	4.35	0.1624	0.0615	2.64
Constant	6.7153	0.0807	83.24	9.1395	0.1290	70.86	9.8593	0.0364	271.12
Ln Sigma	−0.2193	0.0178	−12.35	−0.5853	0.0315	−18.60	−0.8659	0.0064	−135.69
Sigma	0.8030	0.0143		0.5570	0.0175		0.4207	0.0027	

Table E.2 (continued)

	Physician Assistants			Occupational Therapists			Social Workers		
	Estimate	St. Error	t Value	Estimate	St. Error	t Value	Estimate	St. Error	t Value
Age	0.0680	0.0083	8.23	0.0345	0.0066	5.20	0.0455	0.0016	28.94
Age-squared	−0.0007	0.0001	−7.30	−0.0004	0.0001	−4.57	−0.0004	0.0000	−23.25
Female	−0.1720	0.0223	−7.72	−0.1061	0.0208	−5.11	−0.0368	0.0064	−5.77
More than 4 years of college	0.2610	0.0220	11.87	0.0249	0.0172	1.45	0.1827	0.0050	36.51
2003	0.1138	0.0781	1.46	0.0956	0.0467	2.05	−0.0027	0.0144	−0.19
2004	0.0461	0.0722	0.64	0.0882	0.0454	1.94	−0.0176	0.0118	−1.49
2005	0.0553	0.0700	0.79	0.0357	0.0468	0.76	−0.0168	0.0120	−1.40
2006	0.0737	0.0755	0.98	0.0894	0.0446	2.00	−0.0278	0.0120	−2.32
2007	0.1757	0.0694	2.53	0.1039	0.0414	2.51	−0.0424	0.0117	−3.61
2008	0.1556	0.0702	2.22	0.1379	0.0472	2.92	−0.0128	0.0118	−1.09
2009	0.1328	0.0713	1.86	0.1402	0.0440	3.18	0.0015	0.0117	0.13
2010	0.1297	0.0697	1.86	0.1506	0.0444	3.39	−0.0365	0.0127	−2.88
2011	0.1377	0.0684	2.01	0.1223	0.0404	3.02	−0.0354	0.0119	−2.97
Veteran	0.1754	0.0453	3.87	−0.0148	0.0376	−0.39	−0.0370	0.0217	−1.70
Veteran 1990 to 2001	−0.1237	0.0537	−2.31	0.1454	0.0661	2.20	0.0429	0.0323	1.33
Veteran 2001 to 2012	−0.2424	0.0733	−3.31	−0.0319	0.1432	−0.22	0.1367	0.0390	3.51
Threshold 2	−0.0048	0.0311	−0.15	−0.0182	0.0234	−0.78	0.0568	0.0066	8.66
Threshold 3	0.0326	0.0355	0.92	−0.0368	0.0278	−1.33	0.0731	0.0085	8.63
Threshold 4	0.1213	0.0356	3.41	0.0466	0.0283	1.65	0.2099	0.0081	25.92
Threshold 5	0.1594	0.0373	4.28	0.0203	0.0294	0.69	0.1983	0.0087	22.76
Threshold 6	0.1511	0.0757	2.00	0.0276	0.0692	0.40	0.3340	0.0192	17.40
Threshold 7	0.1148	0.1006	1.14	−0.0789	0.2165	−0.36	0.3404	0.0371	9.17
Constant	9.5527	0.1828	52.25	10.2929	0.1511	68.13	9.4826	0.0335	282.66
Ln Sigma	−0.7366	0.0297	−24.83	−0.9773	0.0353	−27.70	−1.0664	0.0106	−100.84
Sigma	0.4787	0.0142		0.3763	0.0133		0.3442	0.0036	

Table E.2 (continued)

	Non–Mental Health Workers		
	Estimate	St. Error	t Value
Age	0.0868	0.0004	244.42
Age-squared	−0.0009	0.0000	−212.79
Female	−0.2825	0.0010	−276.51
More than 4 years of college	0.2111	0.0011	185.76
2003	−0.0055	0.0036	−1.51
2004	−0.0051	0.0031	−1.65
2005	−0.0107	0.0030	−3.59
2006	0.0023	0.0030	0.77
2007	−0.0360	0.0030	−12.20
2008	0.0075	0.0029	2.54
2009	−0.0128	0.0029	−4.37
2010	−0.0321	0.0030	−10.58
2011	−0.0399	0.0030	−13.41
Veteran	−0.0080	0.0027	−2.93
Veteran 1990 to 2001	−0.0118	0.0045	−2.65
Veteran 2001 to 2012	−0.0045	0.0049	−0.93
Threshold 2	0.1045	0.0016	65.32
Threshold 3	0.1366	0.0020	67.14
Threshold 4	0.2394	0.0018	136.61
Threshold 5	0.2846	0.0021	136.48
Threshold 6	0.3378	0.0049	68.93
Threshold 7	0.4042	0.0063	63.71
Constant	8.9967	0.0080	1121.86
Ln Sigma	−0.4843	0.0021	−233.05
Sigma	0.6161	0.0013	

APPENDIX F
Civilian Earnings of Female Physicians

Lo Sasso et al. (2011) studied the starting salaries of young physicians, in particular, those leaving residency programs in New York State during 1999–2008. Their regressions controlled for specialty training (45 categories), year, year-female interaction, race/ethnicity, citizenship status, foreign medical graduate, allopath (versus osteopath), age, educational debt, obligation to work in health professional shortage areas, principal practice setting, location type, and hours of work devoted to direct patient care. They found no statistically significant difference in starting salary between men and women in 1999, but a highly significant difference in 2008 (2008 dollars). The raw mean salaries in 2008 were $174,000 for women and $209,300 for men, a difference of $35,300. The regression-adjusted salaries had a difference of $16,819— that is, about half of the difference remained despite adjusting for hours of work devoted to direct patient care, specialty, practice setting, etc. The authors suggested several reasons for why the earnings gap changed from a statistical difference of zero at start year, 1999, to a deficit of nearly $17,000 in 2008. They argued that the difference was not the result of discrimination or of family status differences (marital status, number of children) between male and female physicians. Instead, the income difference might have come from "unobserved aspects of jobs taken by women" including "greater flexibility and family-friendly attributes." Female physicians might accept less salary growth in exchange for less chance of being on call around the clock or working night and weekend shifts.

In a cross-sectional study, Weeks, Wallace, and Wallace (2009) found the earnings of female physicians to be approximately 25 percent below those of male physicians for family practice physicians, internal medicine physicians, and pediatricians, each analyzed separately. The estimates controlled for the number of years having practiced medicine, practice ownership status, board certification status, type of degree held (osteopathic [DO] or allopathic [MD]), and international medical graduate status.[1] Baker (1996) analyzed data from a 1991 survey of physicians with two to nine years of practice experience and found that unadjusted income was 29 percent lower for female physicians relative to male physicians. Much of the difference came from male physicians working more hours during the year. To adjust for hours the authors computed earnings on an hourly basis, which showed that women earned 8.8 percent less. (We cannot make a similar adjustment with ACS data because they do not detail hours in excess of 40.) Adjusting hourly income for specialty (13 fields of practice) and practice

---

[1] They also created a longitudinal sample of physicians that were present in all three of these surveys and found female earnings to be about 13 percent below those of males. The longitudinal sample had a total of 1,179 physicians as compared with a total of 16,425 observations in the cross sections. This suggests the possibility that the longitudinal sample might have been subject to unobserved selection bias.

95

setting (ten settings)[2] decreased the women's earnings deficit to 2 percent, and adjusting for all variables led to the finding that male and female physicians earned the same.

---

[2] The specialties were general or family practice, general internal medicine, pediatrics, subspecialty internal medicine, emergency medicine, general surgery, subspecialty surgery, obstetrics and gynecology, radiology, anesthesiology, pathology, psychiatry, and other. Practice settings were solo practice, self-employed; group practice, self-employed; group practice, employee; health maintenance organization; hospital; free-standing care center; medical school; university or college; government; and other.

Abbreviations

ACP	Aviator Continuation Pay
ACS	American Community Survey
ADHPLRP	Active Duty Health Professions Loan Repayment Program
ADSO	active duty service obligation
AMGA	American Medical Group Association
ASP	Additional Special Pay
BAH	basic allowance for housing
BAS	basic allowance for subsistence
BCP	Board Certified Pay
CPS	Current Population Survey
DMDC	Defense Manpower Data Center
DRM	dynamic retention model
ECISP	Early Career Incentive Special Pay
FAP	Financial Assistance Program
FY	fiscal year
GME	graduate medical education
GMO	general medical officer
HPO	Health Professional Officers
HPSP	Health Professional Scholarship Program
ISP	Incentive Special Pay
MSP	Multiyear Special Pay
NCS	National Compensation Survey
OES	Bureau of Labor Statistics Occupational Employment Statistics Survey
PTSD	posttraumatic stress disorder
RMC	regular military compensation
ROTC	Reserve Officers Training Corps
S&I	special and incentive
USUHS	Uniformed Services University of the Health Sciences
VSP	Variable Special Pay
YOS	year of service

References

American Medical Group Association, *2011 Medical Group Compensation and Financial Survey Executive Summary: 2011 Report Based on 2010 Data*, Alexandria, Va., 2011. As of May 16, 2016:
http://www.mgma.com/Libraries/Assets/Store/
8390-Management-Compensation-Survey-2011-Report-Based-on-2010-Data-TOC.pdf

AR—*See* Army Regulation.

Army Regulation 601-141, *U.S. Army Health Professions Scholarship, Financial Assistance, and Active Duty Health Professions Loan Repayment Programs*, Washington, D.C.: Department of the Army, September 19, 2006. As of May 16, 2016:
http://www.apd.army.mil/pdffiles/r601_141.pdf

Asch, Beth J., James Hosek, and Michael Mattock, *Toward Meaningful Military Compensation Reform*, Santa Monica, Calif.: RAND Corporation, RR-501-OSD, 2014. As of May 16, 2016:
http://www.rand.org/pubs/research_reports/RR501.html

Asch, Beth J., Michael G. Mattock, and James Hosek, *A New Tool for Assessing Workforce Management Policies Over Time: Extending the Dynamic Retention Model*, Santa Monica, Calif.: RAND Corporation, RR-113-OSD, 2013. As of May 20, 2016:
http://www.rand.org/pubs/research_reports/RR113.html

Asch, Beth J., James Hosek, Michael Mattock, and Christina Panis, *Assessing Compensation Reform: Research in Support of the 10th Quadrennial Review of Military Compensation*, Santa Monica, Calif.: RAND Corporation, MG-764-OSD, 2008. As of May 16, 2016:
http://www.rand.org/pubs/monographs/MG764.html

Association of American Medical Colleges, "Medical Student Education: Debts, Costs, and Loan Repayment Fact Card," October 2015a. As of May 23, 2016:
https://www.aamc.org/download/447254/data/debtfactcard.pdf

———, "Tuition and Student Fees Reports," 2015b. As of May 16, 2016:
https://services.aamc.org/tsfreports/index.cfm

Baker, Laurence C., "Differences in Earnings Between Male and Female Physicians," *New England Journal of Medicine*, Vol. 334, No. 15, April 11, 1996, pp. 960–964.

Bureau of Labor Statistics, "Handbook of Methods," no date-a. As of May 18, 2016:
http://www.bls.gov/opub/hom/

———, "National Compensation Survey," no date-b. As of May 18, 2016:
http://www.bls.gov/ncs/

———, "Occupational Employment Statistics," no date-c. As of May 18, 2016:
http://www.bls.gov/oes/

———, "Occupational Outlook Handbook: Physicians and Surgeons," December 17, 2015. As of May 16, 2016:
http://www.bls.gov/ooh/Healthcare/Physicians-and-surgeons.htm

Defense Finance and Accounting Service, "Military Pay Charts: 1949–2016," 2016. As of May 16, 2016:
http://www.dfas.mil/militarymembers/payentitlements/military-pay-charts

Department of Defense Instruction 6000.13, *Medical Manpower and Personnel*, Washington, D.C.: U.S. Department of Defense, June 30, 1997.

Department of Defense Task Force on Mental Health, *An Achievable Vision: Report of the Department of Defense Task Force on Mental Health*, Falls Church, Va.: Defense Health Board, 2007. As of May 16, 2016: https://archive.org/details/AnAchievableVisionReportOfTheDepartmentOfDefenseTaskForceOnMental

DoD 7000.14-R—*See* U.S. Department of Defense, Under Secretary of Defense (Comptroller).

DoDI—*See* Department of Defense Instruction.

Gillis, Kurt D., "Physician Practice Expenses by Location," *Policy Research Perspectives*, American Medical Association, Chicago, Ill., 2009.

GoArmy.com, "Army Medicine," no date. As of May 16, 2016: http://www.goarmy.com/amedd/education/hpsp.html

Gray, Bradley M., and James E. Grefer, "Career Earnings and Retention of U.S. Military Physicians," *Defense and Peace Economics*, Vol. 23, No. 1, 2012, pp. 51–76.

Hogan, Paul F., Kim Darling, Patrick Mackin, Joseph Mundy, Meredith Swartz, and John T. Warner, "Analysis of Staffing and Special and Incentive Pays in Selected Communities," in U.S. Department of Defense, *Report of the Eleventh Quadrennial Review of Military Compensation, Supporting Research Papers*, Washington, D.C., June 2012.

Keating, Edward G., Marygail K. Brauner, Lionel A. Galway, Judith D. Mele, James J. Burks, and Brendan Saloner, *Air Force Physician and Dentist Multiyear Special Pay: Current Status and Potential Reforms*, Santa Monica, Calif.: RAND Corporation, MG-866-AF, 2009a. As of May 16, 2016: http://www.rand.org/pubs/monographs/MG866.html

Keating, Edward G., Marygail K. Brauner, Lionel A. Galway, Judith D. Mele, James J. Burks, and Brendan Saloner, "The Air Force Medical Corps' Status and How Its Physicians Respond to Multiyear Special Pay," *Military Medicine*, Vol. 174, 2009b, pp. 1155–1162.

Lo Sasso, Anthony T., Michael R. Richards, Chiu-Fang Chou, and Susan E. Gerber, "The $16,819 Pay Gap for Newly Trained Physicians: The Unexplained Trend of Men Earning More Than Women," *Health Affairs*, Vol. 30, No. 2, February 2001, pp. 193–201.

Mattock, Michael G., and Jeremy Arkes, *The Dynamic Retention Model for Air Force Officers: New Estimates and Policy Simulations of the Aviator Continuation Pay Program*, Santa Monica, Calif.: RAND Corporation, TR-470-AF, 2007. As of May 16, 2016: http://www.rand.org/pubs/technical_reports/TR470.html

Mattock, Michael G., James Hosek, and Beth J. Asch, *Reserve Participation and Cost Under a New Approach to Reserve Compensation*, MG-1153-OSD, Santa Monica, Calif.: RAND Corporation, 2012. As of May 16, 2016: http://www.rand.org/pubs/monographs/MG1153.html

Mundell, Benjamin F., *Retention of Military Physicians: The Differential Effects of Practice Opportunities Across the Three Services*, Santa Monica, Calif.: RAND Corporation, RGSD-275, 2010. As of May 16, 2016: http://www.rand.org/pubs/rgs_dissertations/RGSD275.html

Navy Medicine, "Medical Accessions," no date. As of May 23, 2016: http://www.med.navy.mil/Accessions/Pages/default.aspx

Payscale.com, "Resident Medical Officer Salary (United States)," 2016. As of May 16, 2016: http://www.payscale.com/research/US/Job=Resident_Medical_Officer/Salary

Ritschard, Hans, Jill Carty, Melissa Fraine, and Briana Stephenson, *Retention of Military Behavior Health Providers*, Washington, D.C.: Office of the Assistant Secretary of Defense for Health Affairs, Force Health Protection and Readiness, Psychological Health Strategic Operations, July 20, 2011.

Robiner, William N., "The Mental Health Professions: Workforce Supply and Demand, Issues, and Challenges," *Clinical Psychology Review*, 26: 600–625, 2006.

SalaryExpert.com, "Medical Resident Salary in United States," 2016. As of May 16, 2016: https://www.salaryexpert.com/SalarySurveyData/Job=medical-resident/Salary

Seabury, Seth A., Anupam B. Jena, and Amitabh Chandra, "Trends in the Earnings of Health Care Professionals in the United States, 1987–2010," *Journal of the American Medical Association*, Vol. 308, No. 20, November 28, 2012, pp. 2083–2085.

Train, Kenneth, *Discrete Choice Methods with Simulation*, 2nd ed., Cambridge, Mass.: Cambridge University Press, 2009. As of May 16, 2016:
http://eml.berkeley.edu/books/choice2.html

U.S. Air Force, "Healthcare Professionals: Caring for Those Protecting the Nation—Training and Education," no date. As of May 23, 2016:
https://www.airforce.com/careers/specialty-careers/healthcare/training-and-education

U.S. Army Recruiting Command, *FY 2011 Army Medical Department Recruiting Guide*, Fort Knox, Ky., November 10, 2010. As of May 16, 2016:
http://ermc.amedd.army.mil/landstuhl/AMEDDFY11GuideV1.pdf

———, *FY 2014 Army Medical Department Recruiting Guide*, Fort Knox, Ky., November 18, 2013. As of May 16, 2016:
http://rhce.amedd.army.mil/landstuhl/Army_Medical_Department_Recruiting_Program_Guide.pdf

U.S. Census Bureau, "American Community Survey," no date-a. As of May 16, 2016:
https://www.census.gov/programs-surveys/acs/

———, "Current Population Survey," no date-b. As of May 19, 2016:
http://www.census.gov/programs-surveys/cps.html

U.S. Department of Defense, "Military Compensation: Different Types of BAH," no date. As of May 16, 2016:
http://militarypay.defense.gov/PAY/ALLOWANCES/BAH_TYPES.ASPX

———, "Fiscal Year 2000 Medical Officer Special Pay Plan," memorandum, August 8, 1999.

———, *DoD Financial Management Regulation*, Volume 7A, Chapter 5, Special Pay for Medical Officers, Washington, D.C., November 2008.

U.S. Department of Defense, Department of the Air Force, Department of the Navy, and Department of the Army, *HPSP Medical Student Survival Guide: A Guide to the Finer Points of Making the Best of the Department of Defense Health Professions Scholarship Program*, 2nd ed., Washington, D.C., 2013.

U.S. Department of Defense, Office of the Under Secretary of Defense for Personnel and Readiness, *Military Compensation Background Papers*, 6th ed., Washington, D.C., May 2005.

———, *Selected Military Compensation Tables*, Washington, D.C., January 1, 2009.

U.S. Department of Defense, Office of the Assistant Secretary of Defense for Reserve Affairs, *Official Guard and Reserve Manpower Strength and Statistics, FY 2009 Summary*, Washington, D.C., 2010.

U.S. Department of Defense, Under Secretary of Defense (Comptroller), *Department of Defense Financial Management Regulation, Vol. 7A: Military Pay Policy—Active Duty and Reserve Pay*, DoD 7000.14-R, Washington, D.C., 2015.

Uniformed Services University of the Health Sciences, *Catalog 2008–2010*, Bethesda, Md., 2007.

Weeks, William B., Tanner A. Wallace, and Amy E. Wallace, "How Do Race and Sex Affect the Earnings of Primary Care Physicians?" *Health Affairs*, Vol. 28, No. 2, March–April 2009, pp. 557–566.